GUITAR METHOD 1

by AARON STANG

Everyone who begins an instrument—whether a child, teenager, or adult—has one thing in common: they are excited and looking forward to an enjoyable new experience. This method has been designed to encourage that enthusiasm by providing a carefully thought-out, musical, and fun way to learn. The musical examples represent all styles from folk to rock, reflecting the diverse interests of most guitarists. Tablature is used as an aid in learning new material, and suggested accompaniment parts have been included, enabling the teacher to play along and making the lesson more enjoyable for all (accompaniment parts are included on the accompanying recording as well). If you're learning on your own, the included recording will be invaluable; always learn what something sounds like before attempting to play it. This new Complete Edition combines the contents of the immensely successful *21st Century Guitar Method, Book 1*, with two of its most popular supplements—the *Theory Workbook* and five additional pop songs from the *Song Trax* supplement.

A Very Special Thanks

...to my wife, Audrey, for her unswerving support,
...to Sandy Feldstein, without whose suggestions and guidance this book would not have been possible,
...to Dan Warner for contributing his talent to the project,
...to Richard Hoover of the Santa Cruz Guitar Company and Tom Anderson of Tom Anderson Guitars for the use of their amazing instruments.

D1403969

This book is dedicated to my daughter, Kelsey Rae.
Photography: Robert Santos
Recording: Ray Lyon, Aaron Stang and Dan Warner

ISBN-10: 0-7579-0946-9
ISBN-13: 978-0-7579-0946-7

Contents

The Guitar

Electric

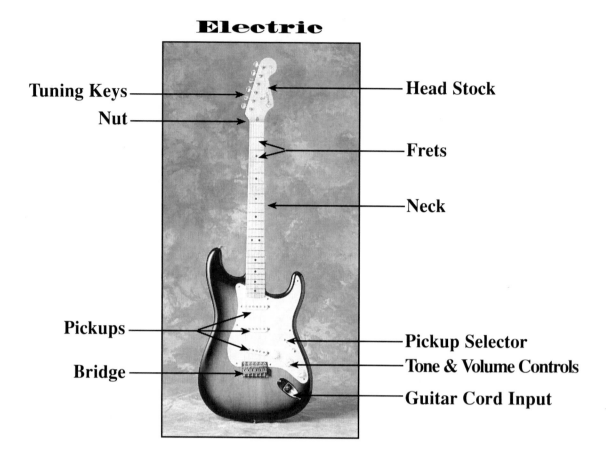

Tuning Keys ——
Nut ——

Head Stock

Frets

Neck

Pickups ——
Bridge ——

Pickup Selector
Tone & Volume Controls
Guitar Cord Input

Steel String Acoustic

Nylon String Acoustic

Although any guitar can be used for virtually any kind of music, the **electric guitar** is commonly used in popular music (Rock, Country, Jazz, etc.), especially when playing with a band. The electric guitar is usually played with a pick.

The **steel string guitar** is perfect for strumming and accompanying yourself. It can be played with a pick or finger-style

The **nylon string guitar** is almost always played with fingers and is ideal for solo and classical guitar styles.

Technique

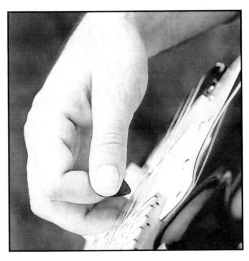

The pick should be held firmly between the thumb and index finger.

The thumb should be placed behind the neck. The fingers should be placed right behind the frets, not on top of, or in between them.

Sitting Position

Classic Position

Standing Position

Tuning The Guitar

Electronic Tuners:

Many brands of small, battery operated tuners, similar to the one shown below, are available. Simply follow the instructions supplied with your tuner.

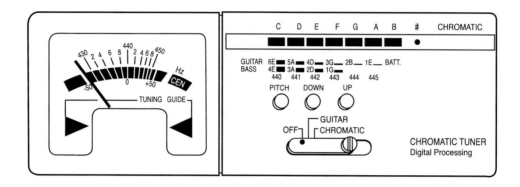

Tuning the Guitar to a piano:

One of the easiest ways to tune a guitar is to a piano keyboard. The six strings of the guitar are tuned to the keyboard notes shown in the following diagram:

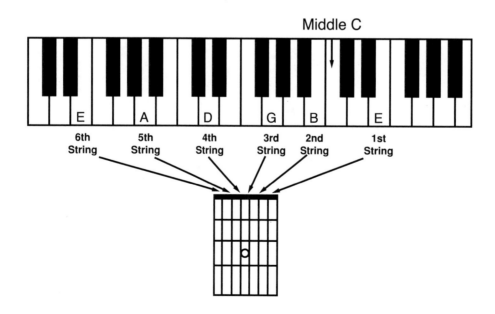

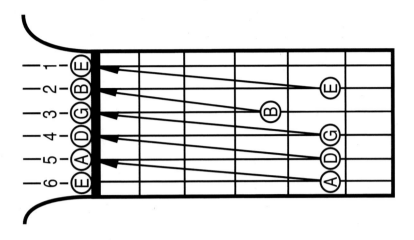

Tuning the Guitar to Itself (Relative Tuning):

1. Tune the 6th string to *E* on the piano (or some other fixed pitch instrument). You can also use a pitch pipe or an electronic guitar tuner

2. Depress the 6th string at the 5th fret. Play it and you will hear the note *A*, which is the same note as the 5th string open. Turn the 5th string tuning key until the pitch of the 5th string matches that of the 6th string.

3. Depress the 5th string at the 5th fret. Play it and you will hear the note *D*, which is the same note as the 4th string open. Turn the 4th string tuning key until the pitch of the 4th string matches that of the 5th string.

4. Depress the 4th string at the 5th fret. Play it and you will hear the note *G*, which is the same note as the 3rd string open. Turn the 3rd string tuning key until the pitch of the 3rd string matches that of the 4th string.

5. Depress the 3rd string at the 4th fret. Play it and you will hear the note *B*, which is the same note as the 2nd string open. Turn the 2nd string tuning key until the pitch of the 2nd string matches that of the 3rd string.

6. Depress the 2nd string at the 5th fret. Play it and you will hear the note *E*, which is the same note as the 1st string open. Turn the 1st string tuning key until the pitch of the 1st string matches that of the 2nd string.

Music Notation

There are seven natural notes. They are named for the first seven notes of the alphabet: A B C D E F G. After G, we begin again with A.

Music is written on a **staff.** The staff consists of five lines with four spaces between the lines:

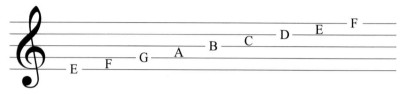

At the beginning of the staff is a treble or G clef. (The treble clef is known as the G clef because it encircles the 2nd line G.) The clef determines the location of notes on the staff. All guitar music is written on a treble clef.

The notes are written on the staff in alphabetical order. The first line is E:

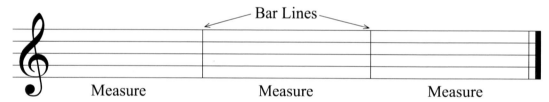

Notes can extend above, and below, the treble clef. When they do, **ledger lines** are added. Following is the approximate range of the guitar from the lowest note, open sixth string "E," to "B" on the first string, 17th fret.

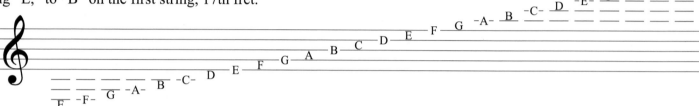

The staff is divided into *measures* by *bar lines*. A heavy double bar line marks the end of the music:

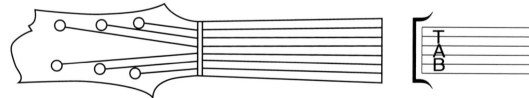

Tablature is a type of music notation that is specific to the guitar; its use dates back to the 1600's. Tablature illustrates the location of notes on the neck of the guitar. Tablature is usually used in conjunction with a music staff. The notes and rhythms are indicated in the music staff; the tablature shows where those notes are played on the guitar.

The location of any note is indicated by the placement of fret numbers on the strings. Tablature is usually used in conjunction with a music staff. The notes and rhythms are indicated in the music staff; the tablature shows where those notes are played on the guitar.

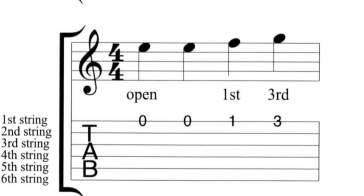

In this book, tablature will be used with all new notes and fingerings. "Tab" will also be used on all pop songs and as an aid to learning the more challenging arrangements; thereby making the learning process easier and more fun.

Rhythm Notation And Time Signatures

At the beginning of every song is a time signature. $\frac{4}{4}$ is the most common time signature:

4 FOUR COUNTS TO A MEASURE
4 A QUARTER NOTE RECEIVES ONE COUNT

The top number tells you how many counts per measure.
The bottom number tells you which kind of note receives one count.

The time value of a note is determined by three things:

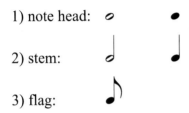

1) note head:

2) stem:

3) flag:

o This is a whole note. The note head is open and has no stem. In $\frac{4}{4}$ time, a whole note receives 4 counts.

This is a half note. It has an open note head and a stem. A half note receives 2 counts.

This is a quarter note. It has a solid note head and a stem. A quarter note receives 1 count.

This is an eighth note. It has a solid note head and a stem with a flag attached. An eighth note receives 1/2 count.

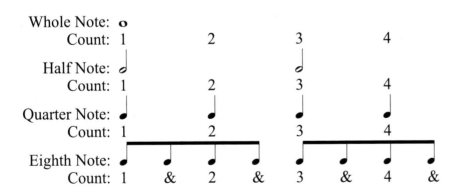

Whole Note: o			
Count: 1	2	3	4
Half Note:			
Count: 1	2	3	4
Quarter Note:			
Count: 1	2	3	4
Eighth Note:			
Count: 1 & 2 &	3 & 4 &		

Count out loud and clap the rhythm to this excerpt from *Jingle Bells.*

Four Counts Per Measure

A Quarter Note Receives One Count

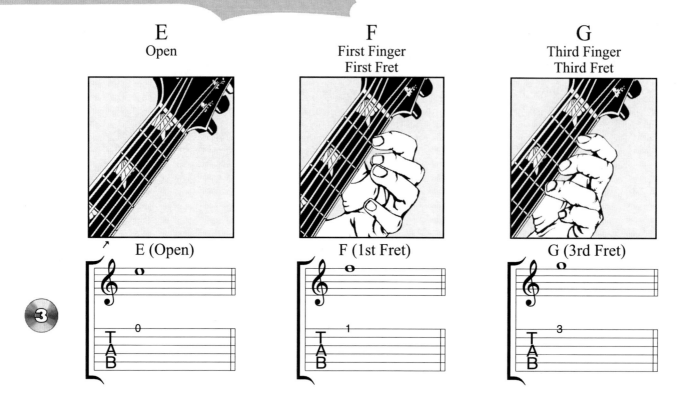

E
Open

F
First Finger
First Fret

G
Third Finger
Third Fret

E (Open)

F (1st Fret)

G (3rd Fret)

Important:

A whole note gets 4 counts: 𝗈 = 4 counts

A half note gets 2 counts: ♩ = 2 counts

A quarter note gets 1 count: ♩ = 1 count

Play all notes with a downstroke (⊓).
(Strike the string with a downward attack of the pick.)

1 Whole Notes:

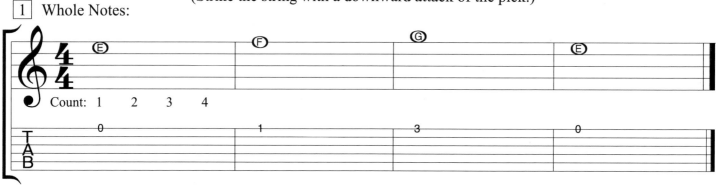

Count: 1   2   3   4

Play slowly, with a steady beat.

2 Half Notes:

Count: 1   2   3   4

Say note names aloud.

3 Quarter Notes:

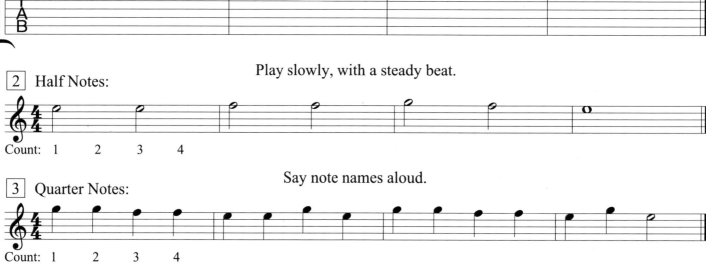

Count: 1   2   3   4

10

Note: Throughout the book, gray chord symbols are for teacher accompaniment.

Folk Song

A.S.

Suggested Teacher Accompaniment:

Flamenco Fantasy

A.S.

Always count with a steady beat—like the ticking of a clock.
Don't slow down, speed up or pause.

The Blues Beat

A.S.

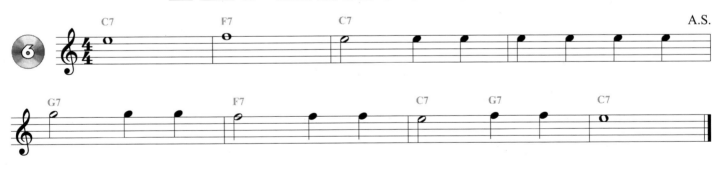

Suggested Teacher Accompaniment:

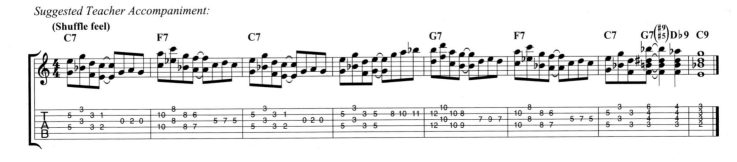

The Notes on the Second String

B
Open

C
First Finger
First Fret

D
Third Finger
Third Fret

B (Open)

C (1st Fret)

D (3rd Fret)

String Combination Study:

Say notes aloud as you play.

Jingle Bells

Brightly

J. Pierpont

Jin - gle bells!   Jin - gle bells!   Jin - gle all the way!   Oh, what fun it

is to ride a one - horse o - pen sleigh. ____ Jin - gle bells! Jin - gle bells!

Jin - gle all the way!   Oh, what fun it is to ride a one-horse o - pen sleigh.

Aura Lee

Slowly

Traditional American Folk Song

As the black - bird in the spring, 'neath the wil - low tree,

sat and piped I heard him sing, sing of Au - ra Lee.

Suggested Teacher Accompaniment:
(Slowly)

The Boogie Shuffle

Medium tempo

A.S.

Suggested Teacher Accompaniment:
(Medium tempo - shuffle feel)

Tied Notes

A curved line connecting two notes of the same pitch is called a *tie*. Play the first note and hold it for the time value of both notes combined. Do not play the second note.

All Tied Up

Mary Ann

Caribbean

All day all night, Mar - y Ann, _____ down by the

sea - shore sift - ing sand. _____ All the lit - tle chil - dren love

Mar - y Ann, _____ down by the sea - shore sift - ing sand. _____

Power Rock

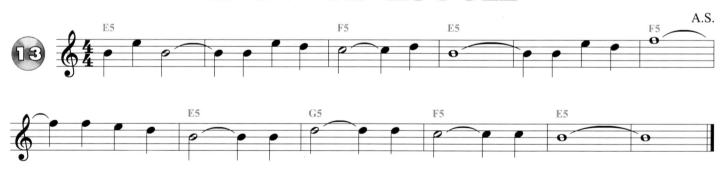

Suggested Teacher Accompaniment:
(Straight-eighth rock)

Not all songs begin on beat 1. Many songs begin with an incomplete measure. *Notes played before the first complete measure are called **pick-up notes.*** The missing beats are usually found in the last measure of the song.

Pick-Up Piece and *When The Saints Go Marching In* both begin on the second beat of an incomplete measure. Count the missing beat (1) out loud and then begin playing on 2.

Pick-up Piece

Count: (1)   2   3   4   1

When the Saints Go Marching In

Traditional Jazz

Fast

Oh   when   the   saints _____ go   march - ing   in, _____ oh   when   the
Count: (1) 2   3   4

Saints   go   march - ing   in. _____   Yes   we'll

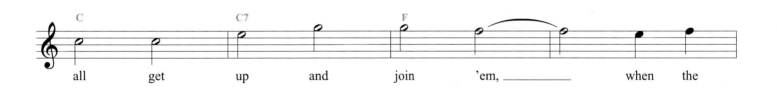

all   get   up   and   join   'em, _____   when   the

Saints   go   march - ing   in. _____

The Notes on the Third String

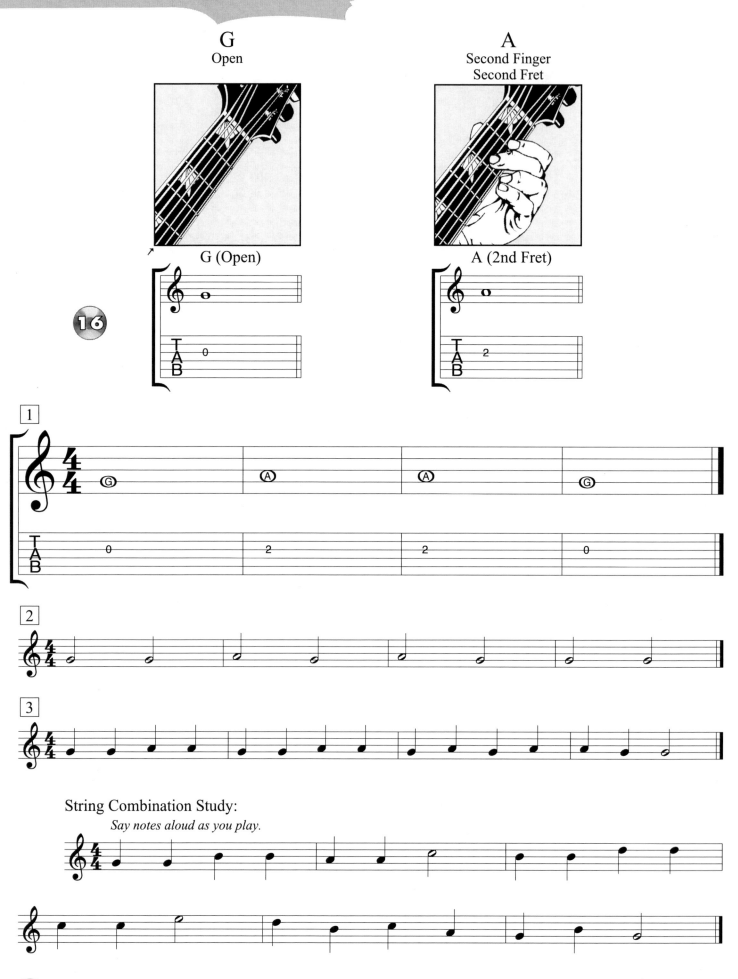

A dotted half note receives 3 counts: 𝅗𝅥. = 3 counts

Note: A dot adds half the value of the note it follows. Since a half note (𝅗𝅥) receives 2 counts, the dot is equal to 1 count. The half note and the dot combined equal 3 counts: 𝅗𝅥 + • = 3

(2) (1)

Oh, Susanna

Gently, a la James Taylor

Stephen C. Foster

17

I come from Al - a - bam - a with a ban - jo on my knee; I'm
goin' to Lou - 'si - an - a, my _____ true love for to see. It
rained all night the day I left, the weath - er it was dry. The
sun so hot I froze to death, Su - san - na don't you cry.
Oh, Su - san - na, oh, don't you cry for me. I
come from Al - a - bam - a with a ban - jo on my knee.

Suggested Teacher Accompaniment:

As Tears Go By was the Rolling Stones' eighth top 40 hit in January of 1966.

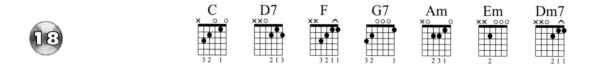

As Tears Go By

Words and Music by
Mick Jagger, Keith Richards
and Andrew Loog Oldham

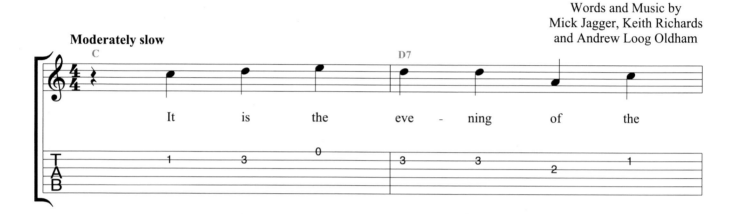

It is the eve-ning of the

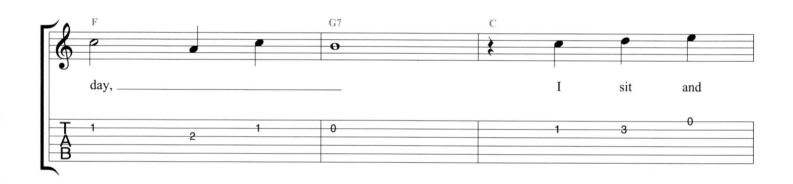

day, _____ I sit and

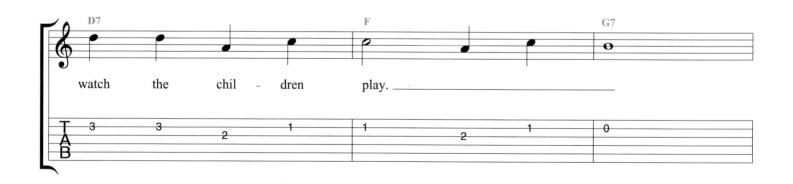

watch the chil-dren play. _____

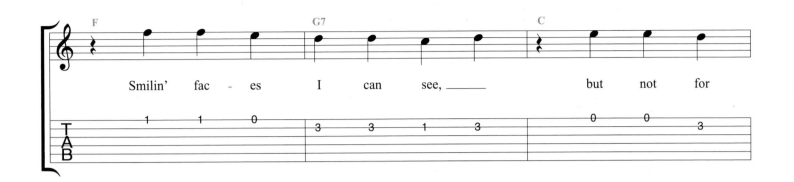

Smilin' fac - es   I   can   see, _____   but   not   for

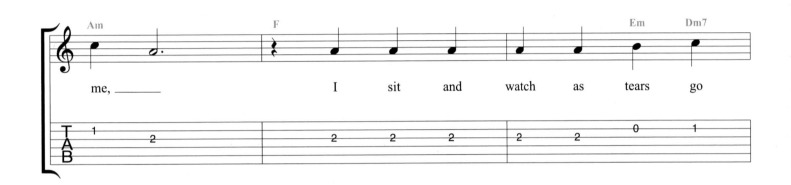

me, _____   I   sit   and   watch   as   tears   go

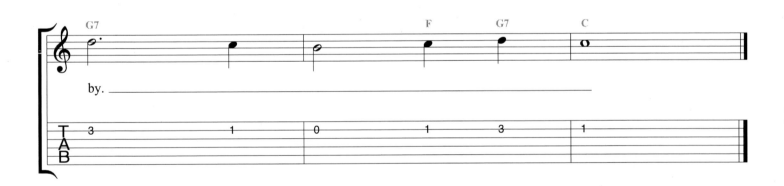

by. _____

New Time Signature: $\frac{3}{4}$

19 $\frac{3}{4}$ Three Counts to a Measure
A Quarter Note Receives One Count

Songs in $\frac{3}{4}$ receive three counts per measure.

Down in the Valley

Kentucky Mountain Folk Song

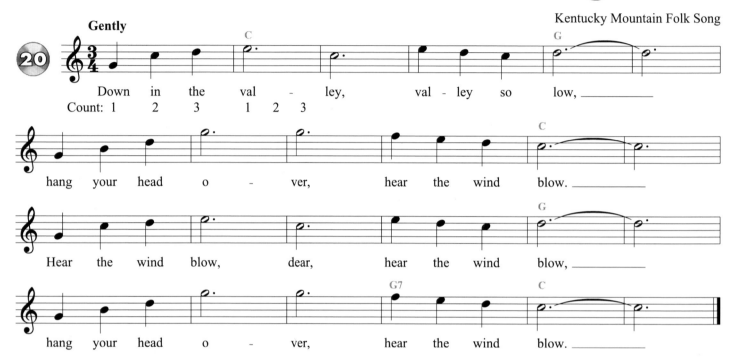

20

Down in the val - ley, val - ley so low, _____

Count: 1 2 3 1 2 3

hang your head o - ver, hear the wind blow. _____

Hear the wind blow, dear, hear the wind blow, _____

hang your head o - ver, hear the wind blow. _____

We Three Kings of Orient Are

Christmas

21

We three kings of O - ri - ent are, bear - ing

gifts we trav - erse a - far. Field and foun - tain,

moor and moun - tain, fol - low - ing yon - der star. _____

Suggested Teacher Accompaniment:
(Moderately, with jazz waltz feel)

22 Repeat signs (:|) tell us to play a section of music again. One backwards facing repeat sign means you should repeat to the beginning:

Repeat back to the beginning.

Red River Valley

Traditional Folk

23 **Moderately**

From this val - ley they say you are go - ing. _____ I will
Come and sit by my side if you love me. _____ Do not

miss your bright eyes and sweet smile, _____ for I
hast - en to bid me a - dieu; _____ but re -

know you are tak - ing the sun - shine _____ that has
mem - ber the Red Riv - er Val - ley, _____ and the

light - ed my path - way a - while. _____
one that has loved you so true. _____

In this next song, allow each note to continue to ring for the entire measure. Keep your fingers curved while playing the fretted notes so that they do not stop the other strings from ringing. Do not lift your fingers from the notes until absolutely necessary.

Singing Strings

A.S.

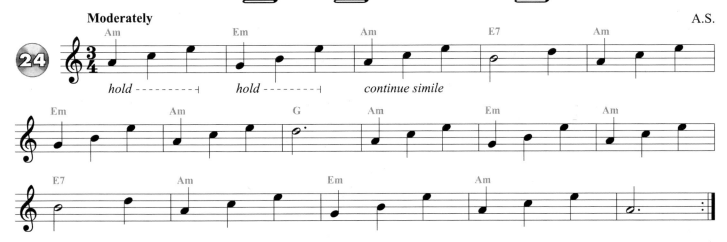

24 **Moderately**

hold --------┘ *hold -------┘* *continue simile*

New Note: A

25 The high A is played on the first string, at the fifth fret, with the fourth finger.

Ledger Lines are placed above or below the staff. The high A is placed on the first ledger line above the staff.

A
Fourth Finger
Fifth Fret

A (5th Fret)

Danny Boy

Irish Folk Song

26 Slowly, with feeling

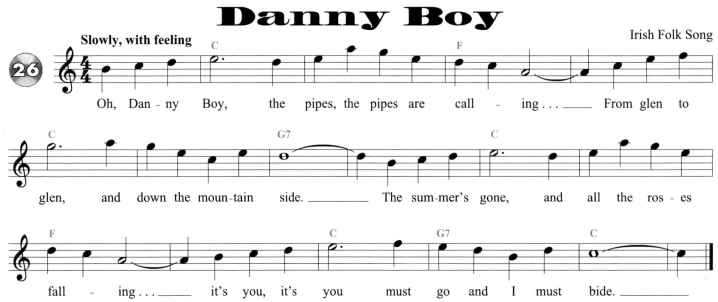

Oh, Dan - ny Boy, the pipes, the pipes are call - ing... From glen to

glen, and down the moun-tain side. The sum-mer's gone, and all the ros - es

fall - ing... it's you, it's you must go and I must bide.

Originally a French operatic song, *Plaisir d'Amour* is so popular that it has passed on into the folk and popular music genres. The song was set to new lyrics and recorded by Elvis Presley as *Can't Help Falling In Love*. It became his 46th Top 40 hit.

Plaisir D'Amour

Jean-Paul Martini

27 Gently

Suggested Teacher Accompaniment:

(Gently)

22

Blue Eyes Crying In The Rain was Willie Nelson's first record to reach the Top 40. The song is a country ballad and should be played slowly, with feeling.

Note: Most printed music for rock and pop guitar includes tablature. In this book, tablature will be included with all pop songs and rock guitar examples.

Blue Eyes Crying in the Rain

Words and Music by Fred Rose

Surf-rock instrumentals became popular in the early '60s. Built around the reverb-drenched sound of Dick Dale, Duane Eddy, and the Ventures, these guitar showcases became major influences on the development of the guitar as a lead instrument in rock. *Telstar,* by the English group The Tornadoes was the number one song in the country, November 1962.

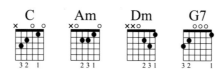

Telstar

By Joe Meek

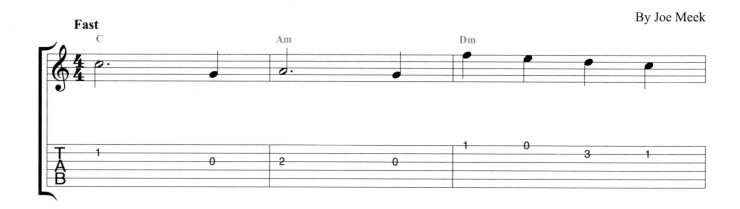

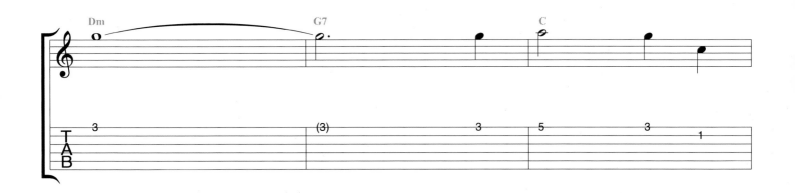

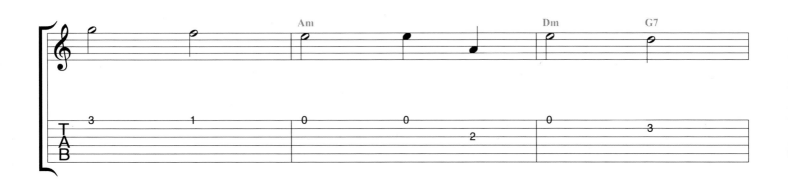

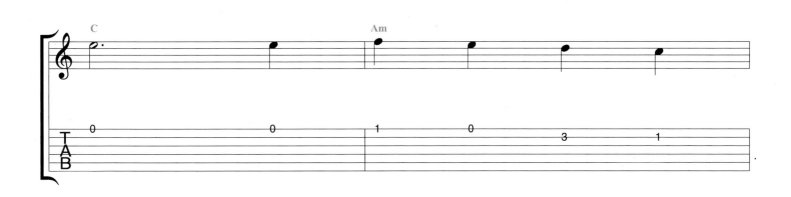

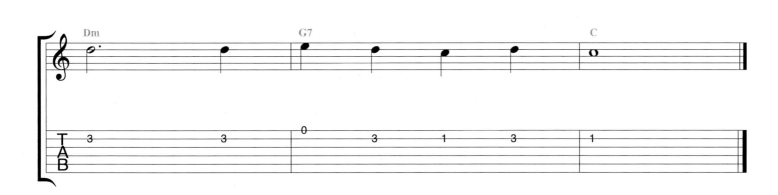

The Notes on the Fourth String

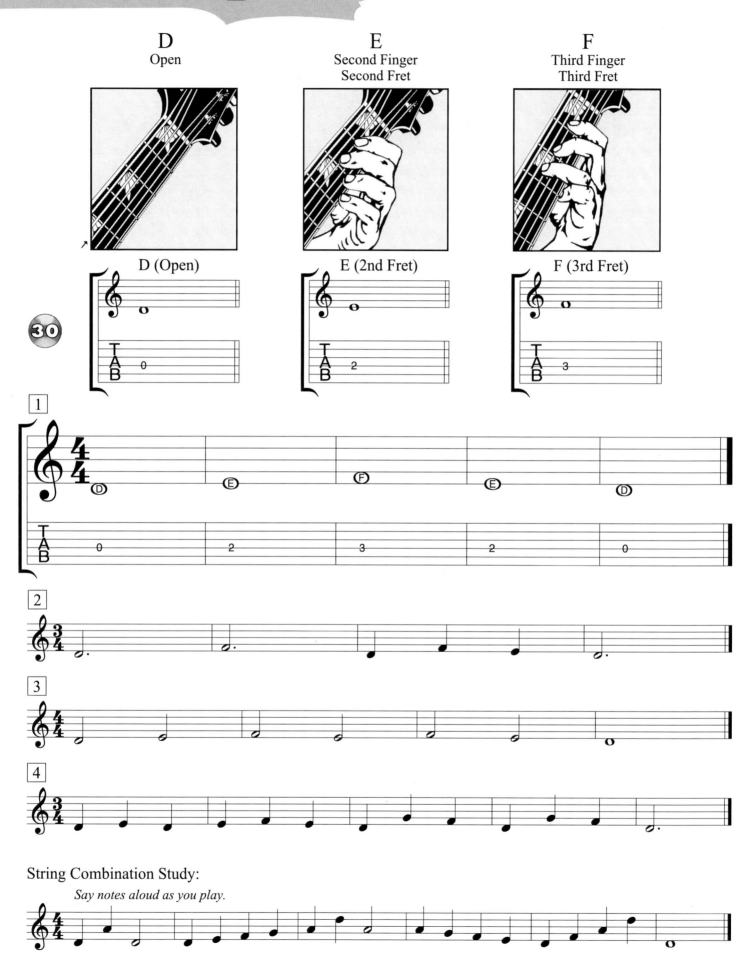

D
Open

E
Second Finger
Second Fret

F
Third Finger
Third Fret

String Combination Study:

Say notes aloud as you play.

Amazing Grace

Spiritual

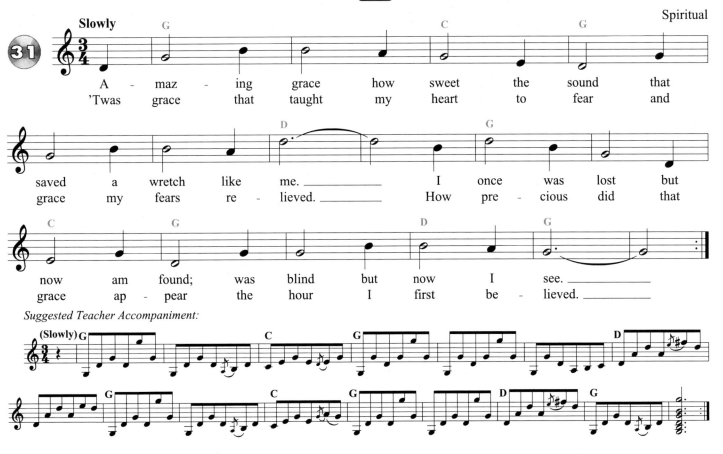

Slowly

A - maz - ing grace how sweet the sound that
'Twas grace that grace taught how my sweet heart to sound fear that and

saved a wretch like me. I once was lost but
grace my fears re - lieved. How pre - cious lost did

now am found; was blind but now I see.
grace ap - pear was the blind hour I first be - lieved.

Suggested Teacher Accompaniment:

(Slowly)

The House of the Rising Sun

Traditional American Folk Song

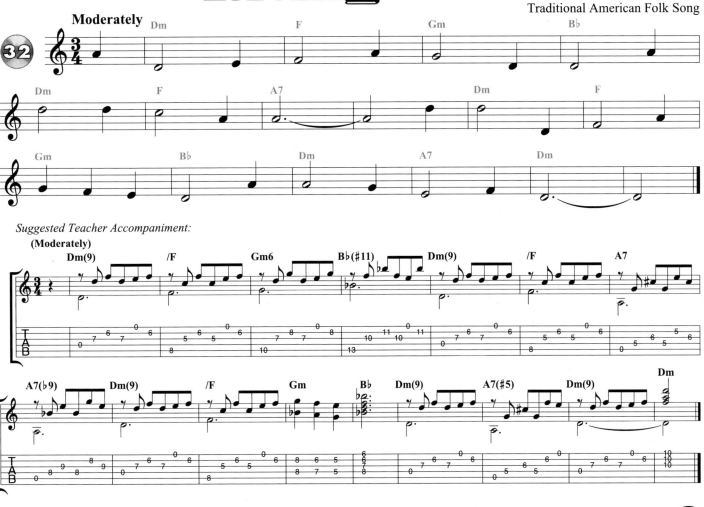

Moderately

Suggested Teacher Accompaniment:

(Moderately)

27

Eighth Notes

33 This is an eighth note: ♪
Two eighth notes equal one quarter note: ♪ + ♪ = ♩

Single eighth notes are written like this: ♪
In groups of two or more, eighth notes are beamed
together: ♫ ♬

Counting Eighth Notes: In $\frac{4}{4}$ time, each
measure is divided into four equal beats.
Eighth notes divide each beat in half. A
beat can be divided in half by saying
"and" in between each count.

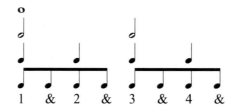

1 & 2 & 3 & 4 &

The Down-Upstroke: The down-upstroke is one continuous movement—a note is played
with a downstroke, then the next note is played with an upstroke *as the pick returns to
playing position.* The pick hand should swing freely from the wrist in a slight arc.

Eighth notes are played with alternating down-upstrokes. Down on the counts (1 2 3 4)
and up on "and."

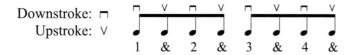

Downstroke: ⊓
Upstroke: V
1 & 2 & 3 & 4 &

Practice this next study until you feel comfortable with both the counting and down/up picking.

Eighth Note Picking Study:

1 (&) 2 & 3 (&) 4 &   1 (&) 2 & 3 (&) 4 (&)   1 (&) 2 & 3 (&) 4 &   1 (&) 2 & 3 (&) 4 (&)

Spy to Spy

Medium

A.S.

34

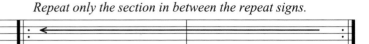

When a section of music falls between two repeat
signs, repeat that section only:

Repeat only the section in between the repeat signs.

Take the repeat once, then continue on to the next section.

Formed in 1961, the Beach Boys are one of the most successful groups in rock history.
They originated the "California" sound with their four-part harmony, and fun, uptempo
rock and roll songs about cars, girls and surfboards. *Surfin' Safari* was the Beach Boys'
first hit single.

Surfin' Safari

Words and Music by
Brian Wilson and Mike Love

The Sharp Sign: ♯

36 A sharp sign (♯) raises the pitch of a note one-half step, a distance of one fret. When a sharp sign is indicated before a note, that note remains sharp for the rest of the measure. The sharp sign is cancelled at the bar line, unless tied.

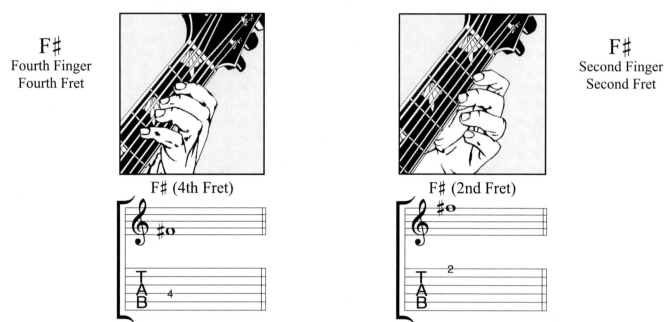

F♯
Fourth Finger
Fourth Fret

F♯ (4th Fret)

F♯
Second Finger
Second Fret

F♯ (2nd Fret)

Earlier, on page 11, we played the first half of *Aura Lee*. Here is the complete version, placed in a different key.

Written in 1861, *Aura Lee* became a favorite of soldiers during the Civil War. The song has such a beautiful melody that, like *Plaisir d'Amour,* it was adapted and recorded by Elvis Presley. This new version of *Aura Lee* became the title song from Elvis' first movie—*Love Me Tender.*

Aura Lee

Suggested Teacher Accompaniment:

Key Signatures

38 Rather than placing a sharp sign before every F, the F♯ can be indicated at the beginning of the line. The sharp sign will be placed on the top line (where the F is written). This is called a **key signature,** and indicates that every F in the song is sharp.

Golden Slippers

Key Signature *(all F's are sharp)*

American Folk Song

Simple Gifts

Shaker Hymn

Suggested Teacher Accompaniment:

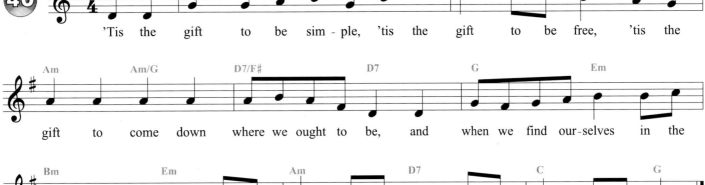

31

The C, G and G7 Chords

A chord consists of two or more notes played at the same time. The C, G and G7 chords can all be played on the first four strings.

Chord Frame Diagrams are similar to tablature. They illustrate how chords are fingered on the guitar fretboard:

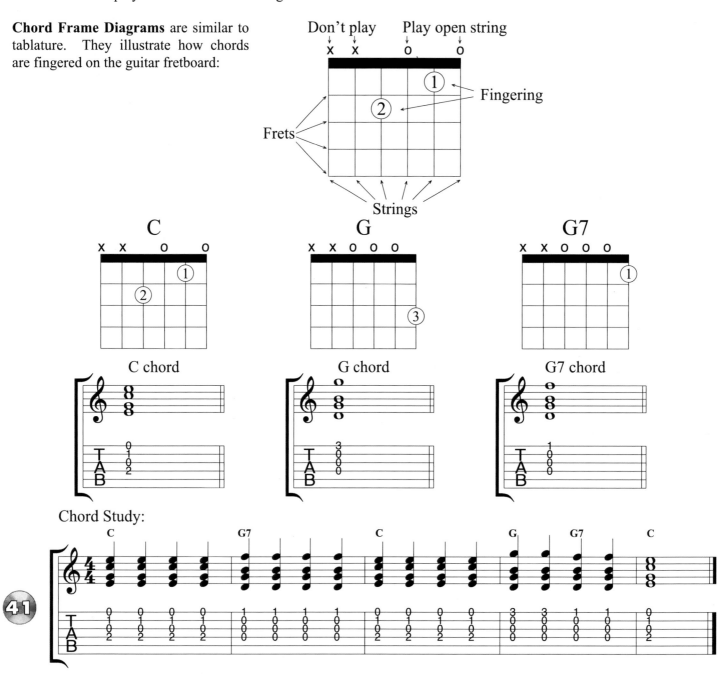

Chord Study:

The next example shows how you can create a good guitar part by holding down a chord and picking each note separately. Use all downstrokes.

Folk-Rock Style

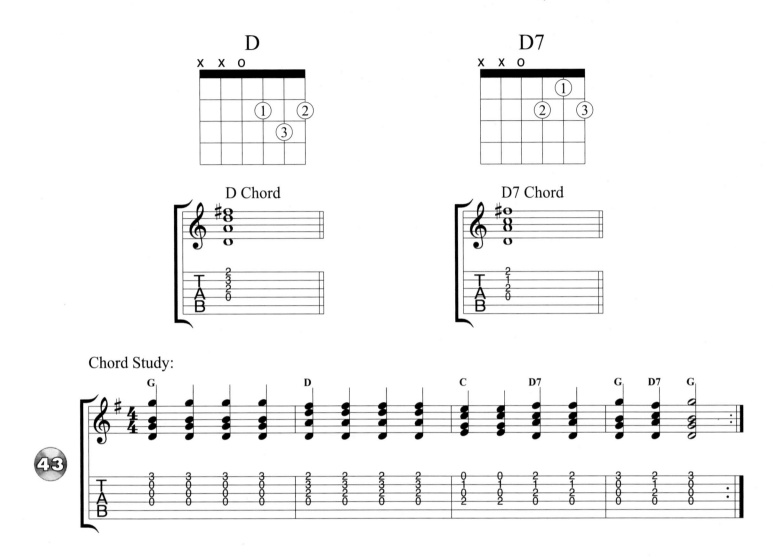

Chord Study:

Often the rhythm of the chord accompaniment is indicated by **rhythm slashes.** The rhythm slashes indicate the strumming pattern.

Rhythm Slashes: ♪ = ♩ = 1 count ♩ = ♩ = 2 counts ○ = ○ = 4 counts

In the next song, the accompaniment part is indicated by rhythm slashes placed above the melody. Learn both the accompaniment and melody parts.

New River Train

Traditional

I'm rid-ing on the new riv-er train. I'm rid-ing on the new riv-er train. It's the

same old _ train that brought me here. _____ It's soon gon-na car-ry me a-way.

*The **Fermata Sign** (⌒) tells you to hold the indicated note or chord beyond its normal duration.*

33

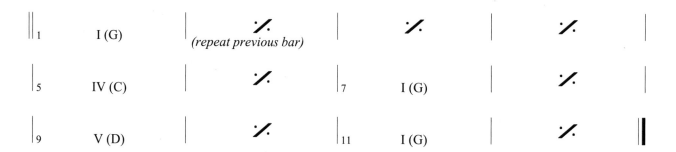

Rock Workshop 101: The Blues Progression

The "Blues" is the most common song form in rock music. The basic blues chord progression is 12 bars long and is built on three chords. In the key of G these three chords are: G, C and D. Often 7th chords are used: G7, C7 and D7.

The three chords in a 12-bar blues are called the I (G), IV (C) and V (D) chords. The blues chord progression always follows the same basic form (with many possible variations):

This next song combines single notes and chords to get the feel and sound of a rock/blues progression. Use all downstrokes for a solid, driving rhythm.

Natural Signs (♮): Notice the natural sign next to the F in bar 4. A natural sign cancels a sharp or flat for the rest of the measure.

The feel of this next song is straight-ahead rock and roll and was first popularized by Chuck Berry. The single note lines are typical of what both the bass player and the guitarist might play on this type of song. This basic pattern continues to be the foundation of many new rock tunes.

Notice the use of the IV chord (C), instead of the V chord (D) in bar 10. This is the most common variation on the basic 12-bar blues progression.

Chuck B. Goode

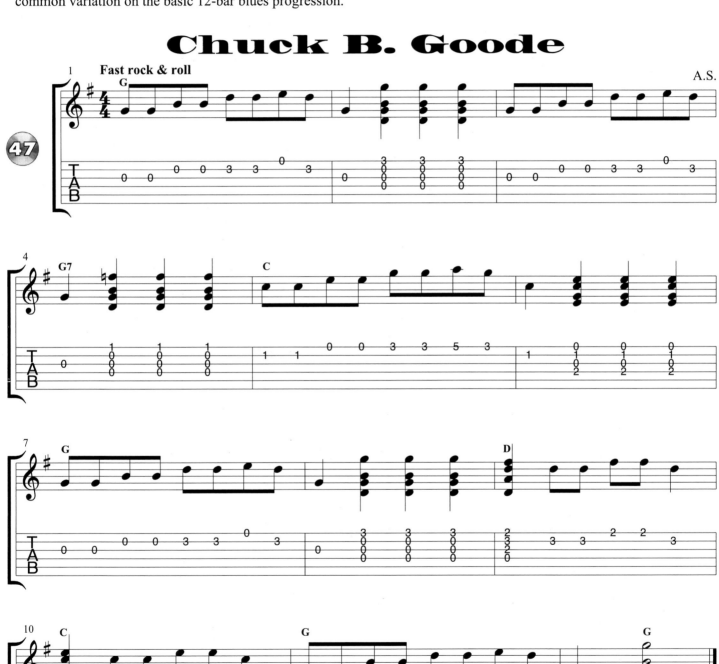

The Notes on the Fifth String:

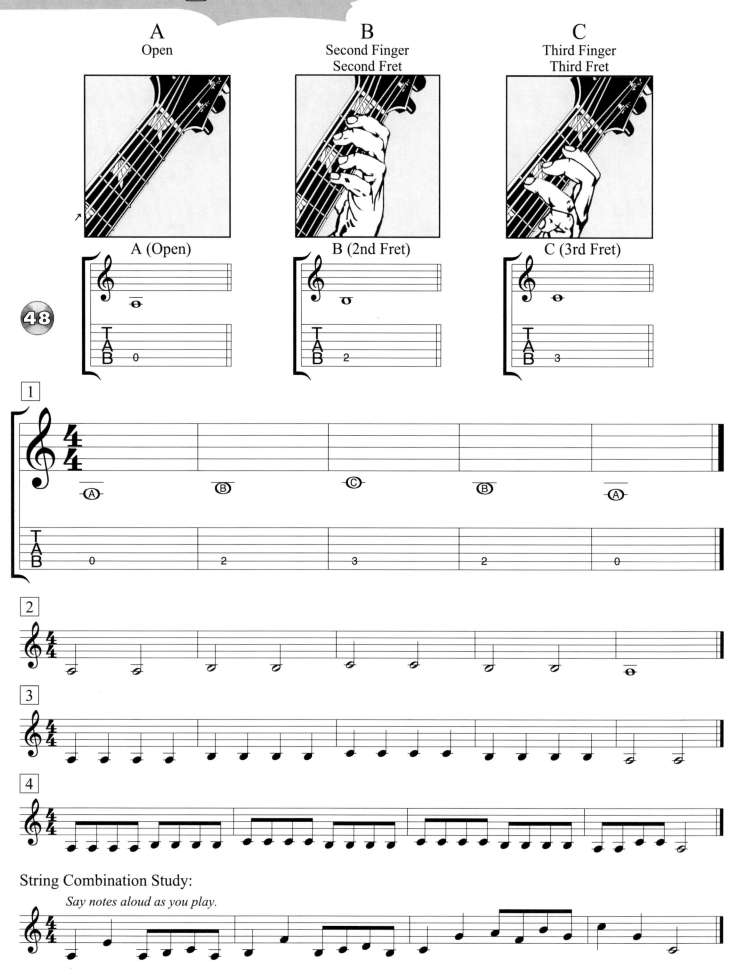

A
Open

B
Second Finger
Second Fret

C
Third Finger
Third Fret

A (Open)

B (2nd Fret)

C (3rd Fret)

String Combination Study:

Say notes aloud as you play.

Brahms Lullaby

Cielito Lindo

The C, A Minor and D Minor Chords

So far you have been playing the C chord on four strings. Here is the full five-string form of the C chord. The A minor chord is also a five-string chord form. The D minor chord uses four strings.

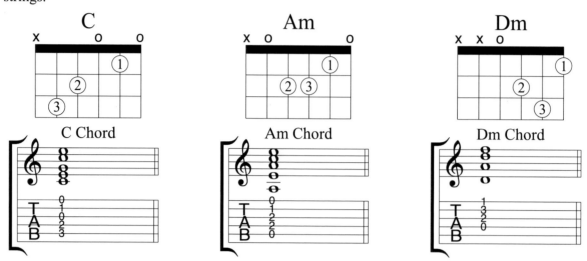

Fingering Tip: When moving from C to Am, keep your first and second fingers in place. Just shift your third finger. When moving from Dm to G7, keep your first finger in place and lift your second and third fingers.

Chord Study:

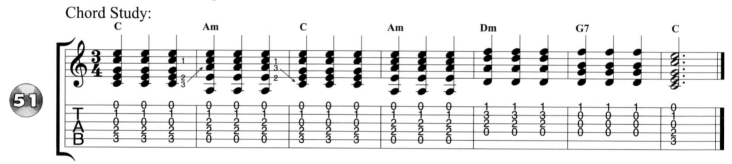

The Roots Of Rock consists mostly of chords played one note at a time. This is called "arpeggio style." Hold each chord down for a full measure. Do not finger each note separately.

Glide Picking: Instead of alternate picking, allow the pick to glide from string to string as shown (all down strokes). For guitar parts like this, glide picking is easier and sounds smoother than alternate picking.

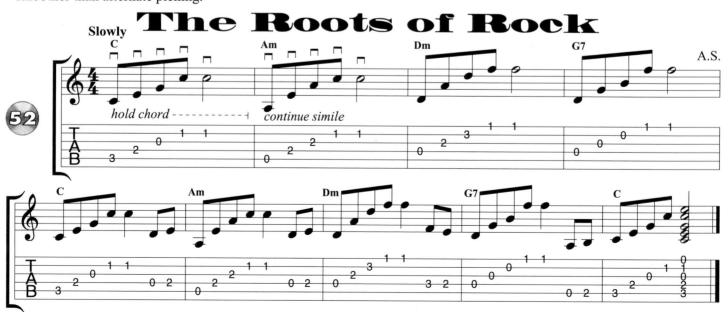

53 This next song uses an eighth-note rhythm to make the strum pattern more interesting. Use an upstroke to strum on "and."

Important Tip: When strumming up and down, always swing your pick hand loosely from the wrist. The pick should pivot in a semi-circle, so that on the up stroke, the top three strings (E, B and G) are accentuated.

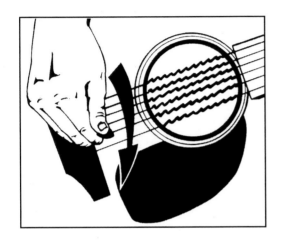
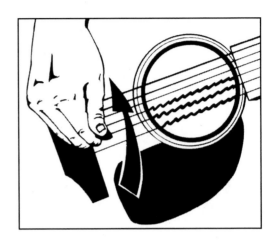

Wrist Rock

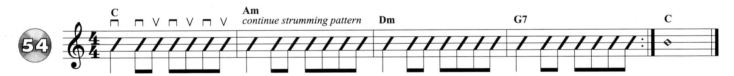

Battle of Aughrim

Over the Rainbow

Over The Rainbow, from *The Wizard Of Oz,* has become one of the most popular songs ever written. Those of you who've been working on your chords will find this one a challenge, but once mastered you will have learned almost all of the basic first position chord voicings. I suggest playing the chords in either a simple quarter-note strum style or eighth-note arpeggios.

Quarter-Note Strum Style: Eighth-Note Arpeggio Style:

Over the Rainbow

Lyric by
E.Y. Harburg

Music by
Harold Arlen

Some - where   o - ver the rain - bow   way   up   high,
Some - where   o - ver the rain - bow   skies   are   blue,

there's   a   land   that I heard   of   once   in a lul - la - by.
and   the   dreams   that you dare   to   dream   real - ly   do   come

true.   Some - day I'll wish up - on   a   star and   wake up where the clouds are   far   be -

I Will Always Love You was written by Dolly Parton in the early '70s. The song was featured in her film *The Best Little Whorehouse in Texas.* Whitney Houston's version of the song, featured in her film *The Body Guard,* became one of the biggest hits of '93 winning several Grammys including "Song of the Year."

The song uses only four chords: C, Am, F and G7. Try playing the accompaniment "arpeggio style" as in the introduction.

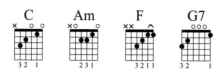

I Will Always Love You

Words and Music by
Dolly Parton

1. If

I should _ stay; well, I would on-ly be in your

2. 3. *See additional lyrics*

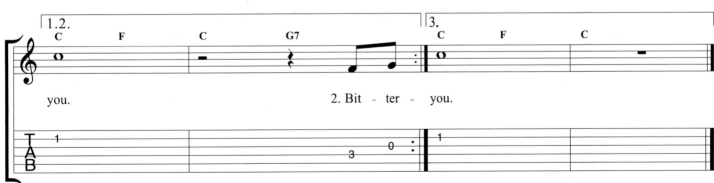

Verse 2:
Bittersweet memories, that's all I have and all I'm taking with me.
Good-bye, oh please don't cry, 'cause we both know that I'm not what you need, but...
(*To Chorus*:)

Verse 3:
(Recite)
And I hope life will treat you kind.
And I hope that you have all that you ever dreamed of.
Oh, I do wish you joy, and I wish you happiness,
But above all this, I wish you love;
I love you, I will always love you.
(*To Chorus*:)

Rock Workshop 102: Power Chords

58 Power chords are the foundation of many blues, rock and metal tunes. Power chords are two-note chord voicings. They are perfect for hard-driving rhythm guitar parts and are often played in unison with the bass line to provide a "big" sound with lots of bottom. Power chords are notated by the letter name of the chord (its root) followed by a 5: A5, D5, etc.

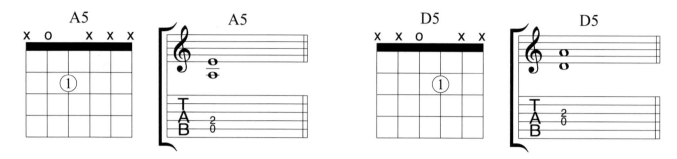

Notice that although A5 is played on the fifth and fourth strings and D5 is played on the fourth and third strings, they both look alike and are fingered alike—with the first finger at the second fret.

Power Study

59

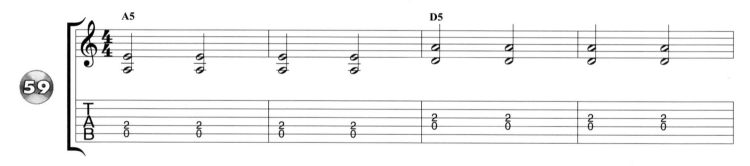

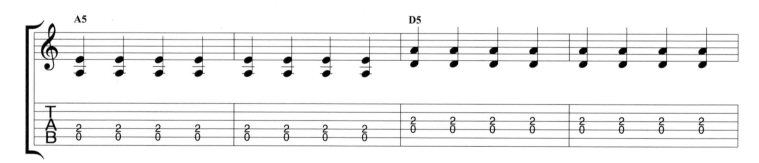

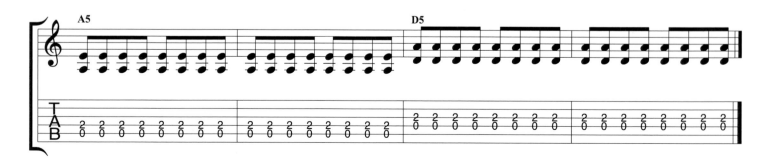

Metalurgy shows how the 12-bar blues form has been adapted to heavy metal; the three chords are A5 (I), D5 (IV) and E5 (V)—more on E5 later. The song is a blues in "A" with a feel reminiscent of Anthrax and Iron Maiden.

First and Second Endings: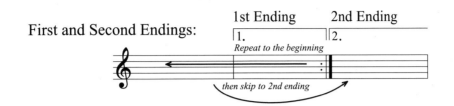

Metalurgy

The Notes on the Sixth String:

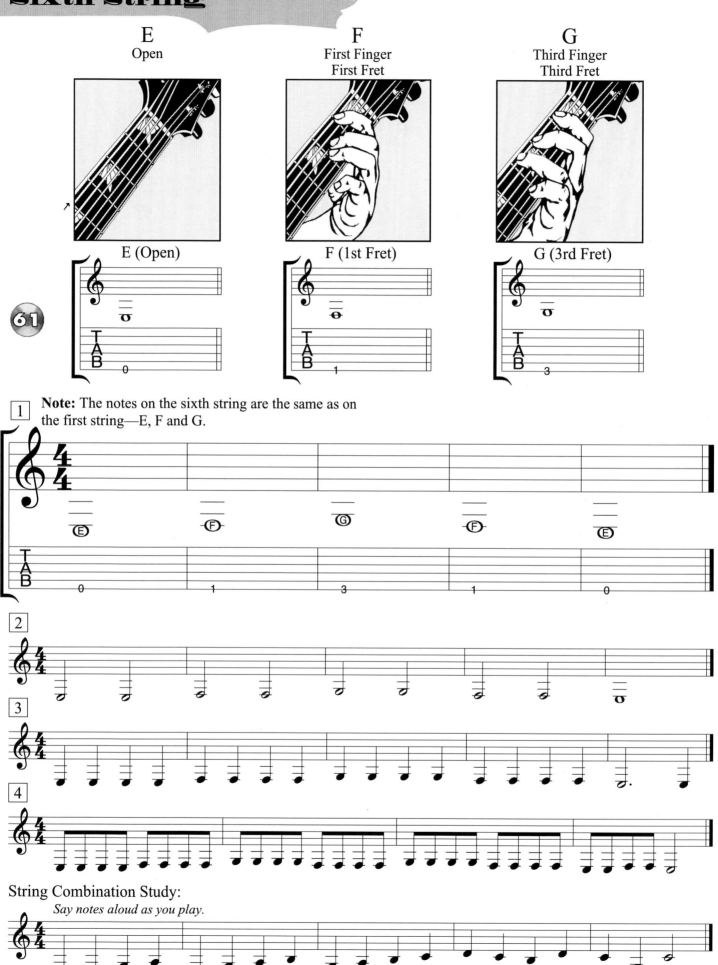

E
Open

F
First Finger
First Fret

G
Third Finger
Third Fret

E (Open)

F (1st Fret)

G (3rd Fret)

1 **Note:** The notes on the sixth string are the same as on the first string—E, F and G.

String Combination Study:
Say notes aloud as you play.

Spanish Serenade

Suggested Teacher Accompaniment:

You've heard variations on this next guitar part hundreds of times, especially in the music of the early "surf" and rockabilly guitarists, like The Ventures, Dick Dale, and Duane Eddy. The song is built on the 12-bar blues form (in E minor). To get a really authentic sound, use an electric guitar on the lead pickup *with lots of reverb.*

Surf-Rock Bass

Roy Orbison began recording in 1956 and had a string of 22 Top 40 records in the '50s and '60s. *Oh, Pretty Woman* was one of his biggest hits. The song was also recorded by the rock supergroup Van Halen. It became one of their biggest hits of the '80s.

Oh, Pretty Woman begins with a classic rock guitar riff.

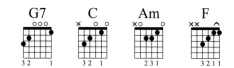

Oh, Pretty Woman

Words and Music by
Roy Orbison and
Bill Dees

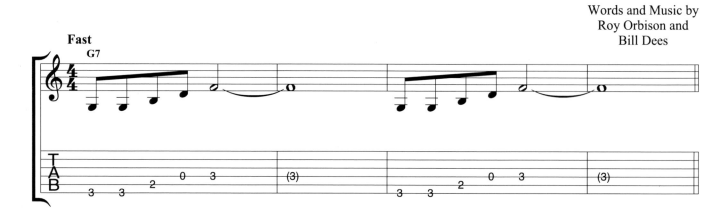

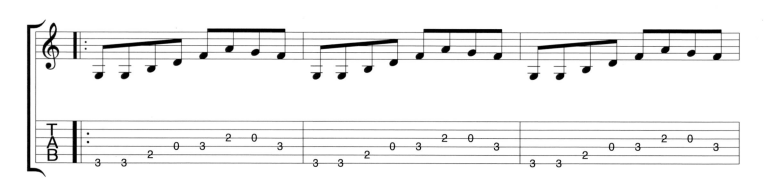

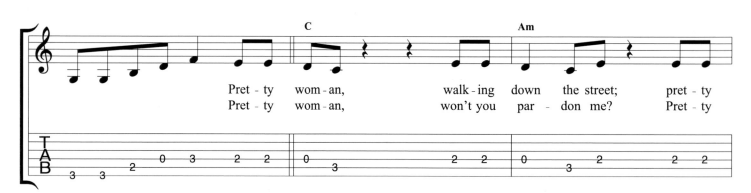

Pret - ty wom - an, walk - ing down the street; pret - ty
Pret - ty wom - an, won't you par - don me? Pret - ty

Oh, Pretty Woman

wom - an, the kind I like to meet, pret - ty
wom - an, I could - n't help but see; pret - ty

wom - an, _____ I don't be - lieve you; you're not the
wom - an, _____ that you look love - ly as can

truth. No - one could look as good as you.
be. Are you lone - ly good just like

1.

2.
me?

Pret - ty wom - an.

Rock Workshop 103: Getting the Feel

 Getting the right "feel" is everything when playing rock guitar. Two techniques that will help you get that feel are: **Accents** and **Palm Muting.**

Palm Mute: Gently lay the palm of your pick hand on the bridge of your guitar. If your hand is too far in front of the bridge, the strings will be too muted and not produce any tone at all. If your hand is too far behind the bridge, the strings will not be muted enough. The palm mute produces a short, muffled, percussive attack which greatly adds to the rhythmic drive and intensity of your playing.

The palm mute is indicated by the abbreviation: **P.M.**

The E5 Power Chord has its *root* on the sixth string. Notice that although each of the three power chords (E5, A5 and D5) are played on different string groups, they all look alike and are fingered alike—with the first finger at the second fret.

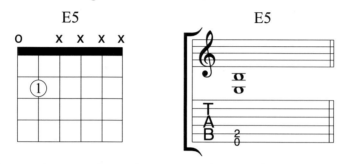

In the following three examples, work on getting a short, percussive attack on the muted chords. Note the contrast between the muted and unmuted sections.

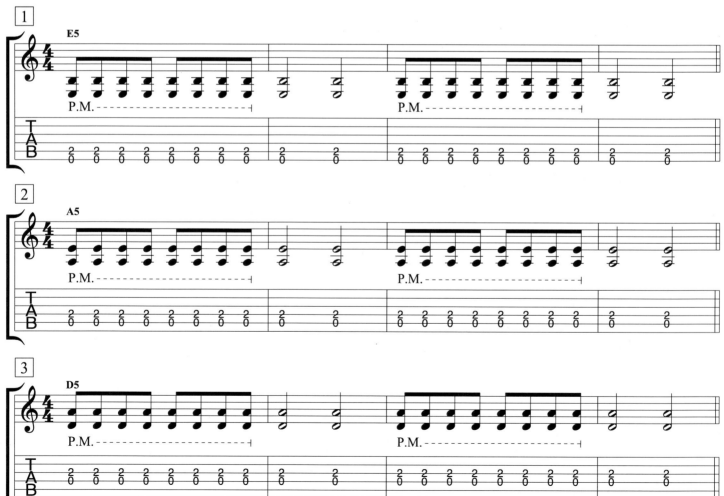

Accents: An accent mark (>) tells you to emphasize a note or chord. The accents in this next example form a pattern which breaks the eight notes in each measure into three groups. You may want to try counting the pattern as shown, until you can "feel" it:

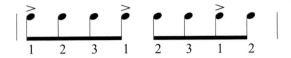

4 Muted rhythm with accents:

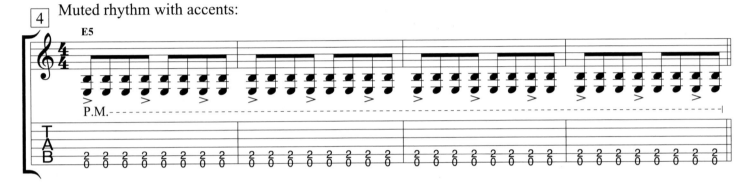

Rock Steady is a 12-bar blues in "A." The three chords are: A5 (I), D5 (IV) and E5 (V). Use the palm mute throughout and the accent pattern where indicated.

Rock Steady

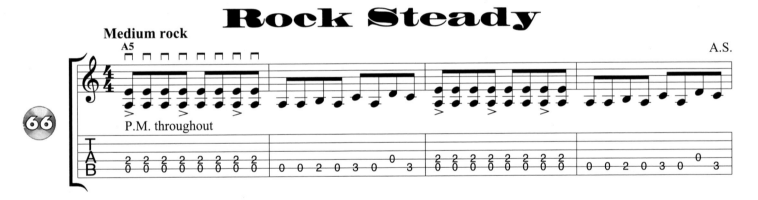

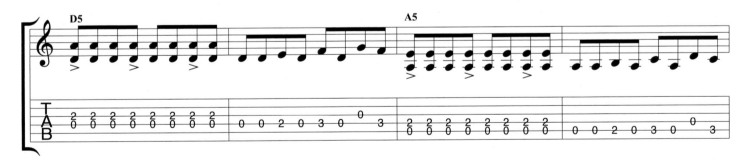

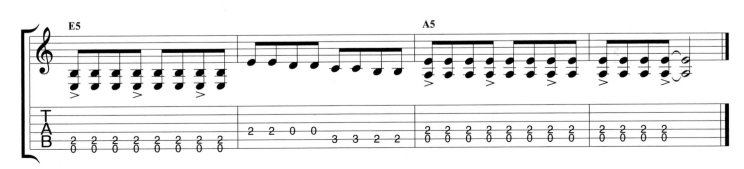

The Full G, G7 and E Minor Chords

Here are the complete, six string chord forms for G and G7, along with a new chord: E minor.

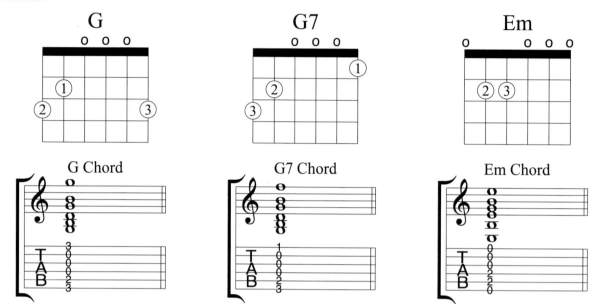

G

G7

Em

G Chord

G7 Chord

Em Chord

67 Notice how similar the G7 chord shape is to the C chord shape. To change between C and G7, simply move each finger to the next string.

To change between the G and D7 chords, slide your third finger along the first string while shifting your first and second fingers.

Chord Study 1:

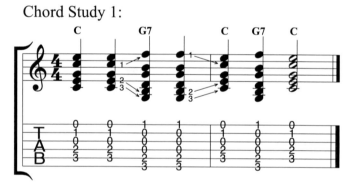

Chord Study 2:

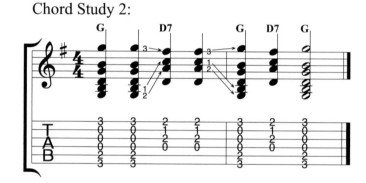

Loch Lomond

Scottish

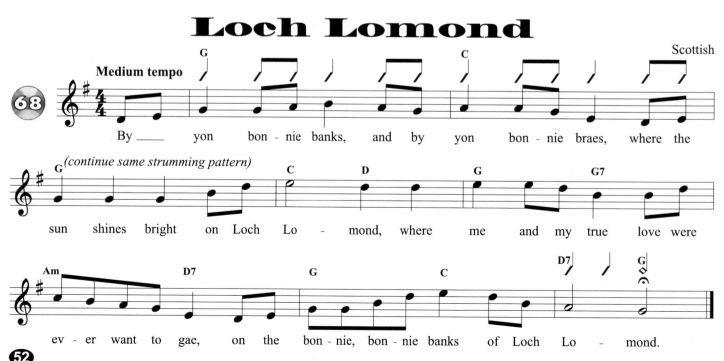

68 Medium tempo

By ____ yon bon - nie banks, and by yon bon - nie braes, where the

(continue same strumming pattern)

sun shines bright on Loch Lo - mond, where me and my true love were

ev - er want to gae, on the bon - nie, bon - nie banks of Loch Lo - mond.

69 The sixth string F♯ is played at the second fret with the second finger:

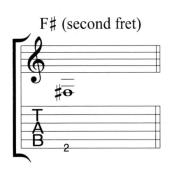

F♯ (second fret)

The next song consists of two sections, labeled ⒜ and ⒝ . The song follows the form:
A A B A. Many pop songs follow this same form. The ⒜ section is played arpeggio style.
The ⒝ section changes to strumming style. This is the kind of rhythm guitar part you
might play on a recording session for a soft rock ballad.

Rock Ballad

Six String Note Review:

Say notes aloud as you play.

Scarborough Fair

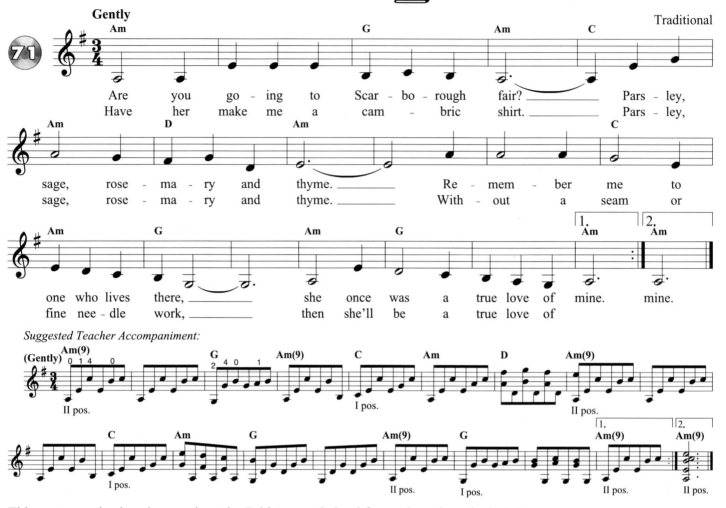

This next song is played arpeggio style. Tablature and chord frames have been included to help with the fingerings.

On Cloud Nine

A rest is a period of silence. Each type of note has a corresponding rest:

Whole Rest: ▬ = o = 4 beats   Half Rest: ▬ = ♩ = 2 beats

Quarter Rest: 𝄽 = ♩ = 1 beat   Eighth Rest: 𝄾 = ♪ = 1/2 beat

When playing a note followed by a rest you should stop that note from ringing. To stop a fretted note from ringing, release the finger pressure on that note. To stop an open string from ringing, you can either gently touch the string with your left hand, or use the palm of your right hand to deaden the note.

Count out loud and tap your foot in the following studies.

Rest & Roll

Count the following exercise carefully. Move your pick in a constant down-up motion. When no note is played on the downbeat move your pick down anyway—only miss the string. This will put your hand in position to play the next note with an upstroke.

Eighth Rest Etude

This excerpt from *A Little Night Music* utilizes both the quarter and eighth note rests. Count carefully and tap your foot on each beat. (The foot should go down on beats 1, 2, 3 and 4 and up on "and.")

A Little Night Music

Medium tempo   Wolfgang Amadeus Mozart

Rock Workshop 104:
The Blues Boogie Pattern

 The blues boogie pattern is based on alternating between the basic two-note power chord and a two-note sixth chord:

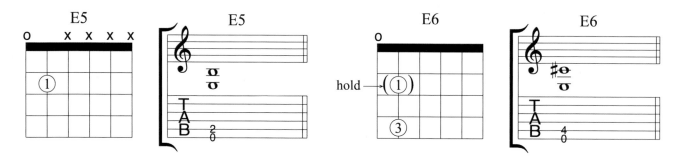

When changing from E5 to E6, keep your first finger on the B as you place your third finger on the C♯. Note: C♯ is at the fourth fret, one fret above C.

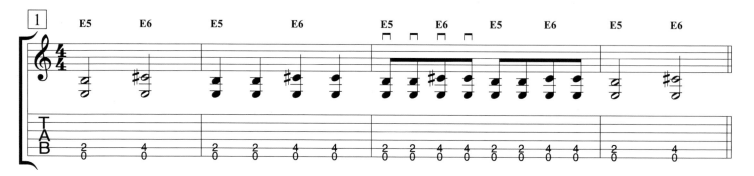

Now try alternating between A5 and A6. When changing from A5 to A6, keep your first finger on E as you place your third finger on F♯:

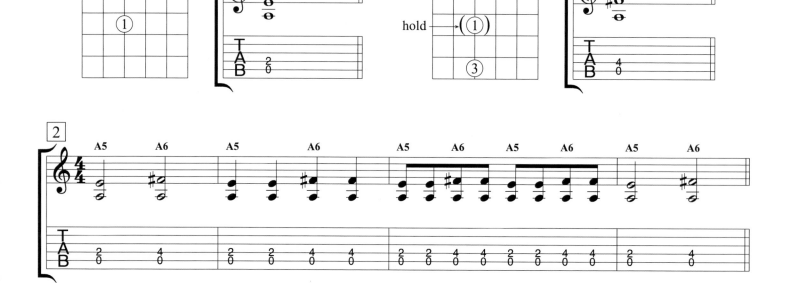

Now alternate between D5 and D6. When changing from D5 to D6, keep your first finger on A as you place your third finger on B. *Notice that you are now playing B on the third string (fourth fret) instead of the second string (open).* On the guitar, most notes can be played in more than one location.

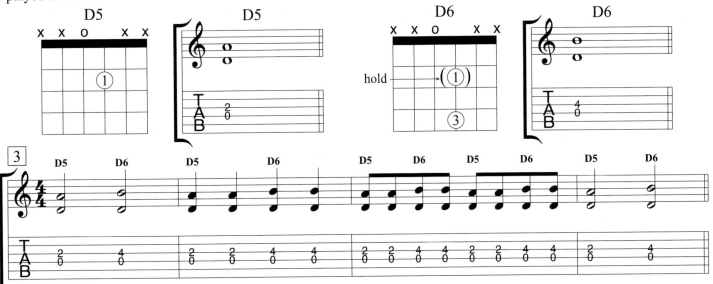

Notice that when alternating E5/E6, A5/A6 and D5/D6 the fingering pattern remains the same—even though each is played on a different string group.

Now, let's combine the three patterns into a 12-bar blues. You've heard this pattern in the songs of Chuck Berry, the Beatles, the Rolling Stones, Eric Clapton, Stevie Ray Vaughan, Van Halen and just about every band that's ever played rock.

The Boogie Progression

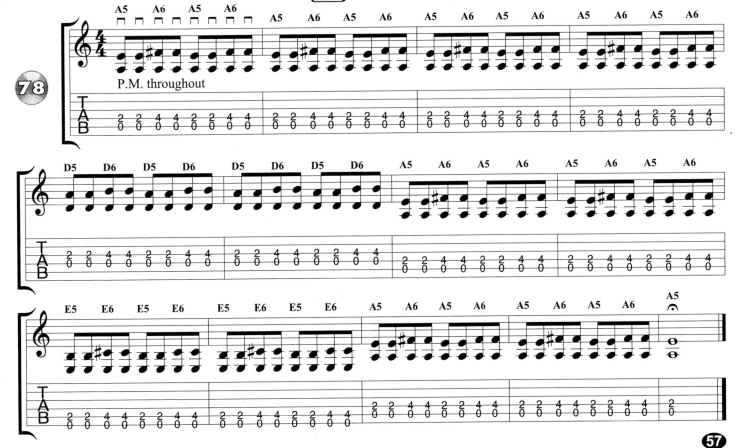

Everything you've studied so far comes together in *Old Time Rock & Roll*. Note that the rhythm guitar part is based on an 8-bar version of the basic boogie progression studied in Rock Workshop 104:

The C♯ found in measures 2 and 6 is located one fret above C: second string, second fret. (The small size notes and tab numbers [called cue size] indicate variations on the melody in the second and third verses.)

Old Time Rock & Roll

Words and Music by
George Jackson and
Thomas E. Jones III

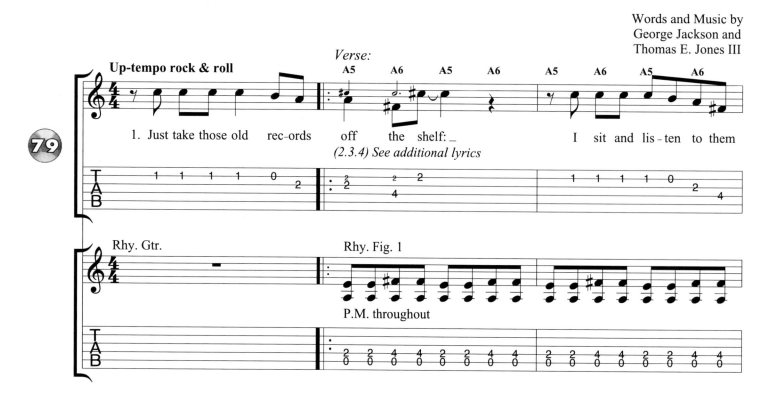

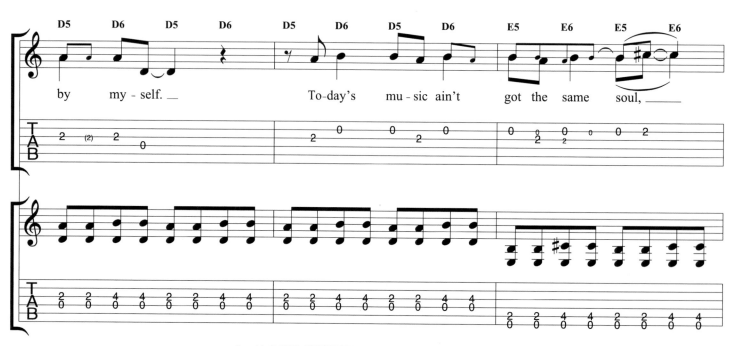

Verse 2:
Don't try to take me to a disco,
You'll never even get me out on the floor.
In ten minutes I'll be late for the door,
I like that old time a rock and roll.
(To Chorus:)

Verse 3:
Won't go to hear 'em play a tango.
I'd rather hear some blues or funky old soul.
There's only one sure way to get me to go,
Start playing old time rock and roll.

Verse 4:
Call me a relic, call me what you will,
Say I'm old-fashioned, say I'm over the hill.
Today's music ain't got the same soul.
I like that old time rock and roll.
(To Chorus:)

Guitar Chord Chart

The following chart shows all of the most commonly used guitar chords.
o indicates an open string. x indicates the string is not to be played.

THEORY
WORKBOOK

Music Notation

Music is written on a five line staff. Between each line there is a space.

Number the lines and spaces:

line #___ →
 space # ___
line #___ →
 space # ___
line #___ →
 space # ___
line #___ →
 space # __1__
line #__1__ →

At the beginning of each staff there is a clef. The treble clef encircles the second line which is the note G. Therefore, it is sometimes called the G clef:

Notes are named after the first seven letters of the alphabet (A through G):

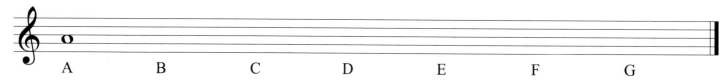

Draw the notes of the musical alphabet:

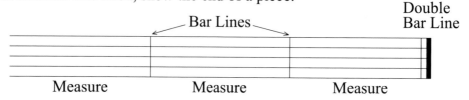

Music is divided into equal parts called **measures.**
Bar lines indicate the beginning and end of measures.

The distance between two bar lines is called a measure.
Double bar lines, one thin and one thick, show the end of a piece.

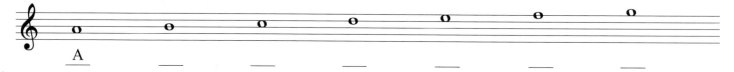

1. Divide the staff into seven measures.
2. Name the notes.
3. End the staff with a double bar line.

At the beginning of every song is a **time signature**. $\frac{4}{4}$ is the most common time signature:

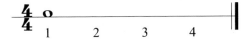

4 Four Counts To A Measure

4 A Quarter Note Receives One Count

In $\frac{4}{4}$ time a whole note receives four beats:

A half note receives two beats:

A quarter note receives one beat:

In the following three exercises, fill in the beats under the notes. Remember, there are four beats in each measure.

Add bar lines in the appropriate places (every four beats). End with a double bar.

Add bar lines (every four beats) then name the notes.

A _ _ _ _ _ _ _ _ _ _ _ _ _ _

Use after page 9.

The Notes on the First String

Name the notes indicated on the treble staff:

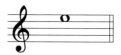  

___ ___ ___

This frame indicates a note played with the _____ finger at the ___ fret of the ___ string. Its note name is _____ . Play the note and say its name.

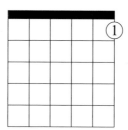

This tablature indication shows that the ___ string is to be played at the _____ fret. It will sound the note _____ . Play the note and say its name.

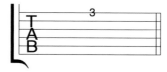

Name the notes indicated in the guitar frames:

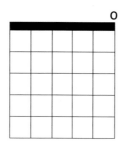 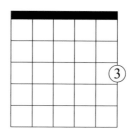

___ ___

Draw the notes indicated in the tablature on the treble staves:

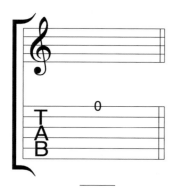 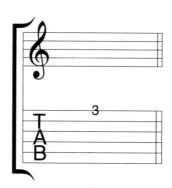 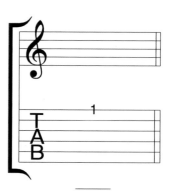

___ ___ ___

Name the notes and play them.

Use after page 10.

Name the indicated notes:

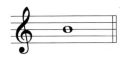 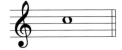 

___ ___ ___

This frame indicates a note played with the _____ finger at the ___ fret of the ___ string. Its note name is _____ . Play the note and say its name.

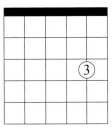

This tablature indication shows that the ___ string is to be played at the _____ fret. It will sound the note ___ . Play the note and say its name.

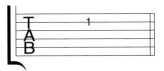

Name the notes indicated in the guitar frames:

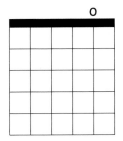 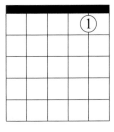

___ ___

Notate in the tablature, the indicated notes:

___ ___ ___

Name the notes and play them.

Use after page 12.

Tied Notes

A **tie** is a curved line that connects two adjacent notes of the same pitch. Hold the two notes as though they are one.

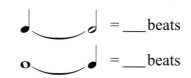

Add the beats of the tied notes:

= _3_ beats   = ___ beats

= ___ beats   = ___ beats

Draw the note that equals the number of beats of the tied notes:

=   =

=   =

Pick-up Notes

The opening measures of "The Saints" contain pick-up notes and ties.

1. Draw the bar lines.
2. Write the counting above the staff.
3. Name the notes below the staff.

Note Review

1. Draw the note indicated on the fret diagram.
2. Place the correct fret number on the correct string in the tablature.
3. Name the note and play it.

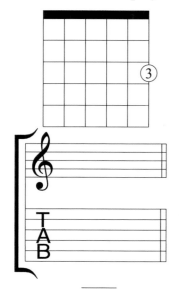
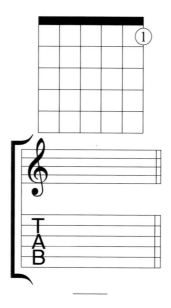
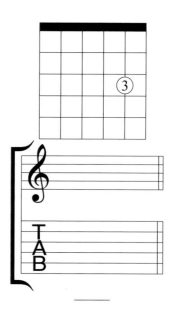

Use after page 14.

Draw the indicated notes:

<u>A</u>

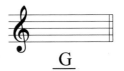

<u>G</u>

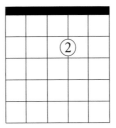

This frame indicates a note played with the ____ finger at the ____ fret of the ____ string. Its note name is ____ . Play the note and say its name.

This tablature indication shows that the ____ string is to be played *open*. It will sound the note ____ . Play the note and say its name.

The note indicated in the guitar frame is: ____

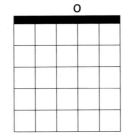

Draw G on the treble staff:

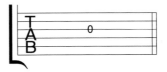

Note Review

For every note indicated in the tablature:
1. Indicate the correct finger, at the correct fret on the diagram.
2. Draw the note on the treble staff.
3. Name the note and play it.

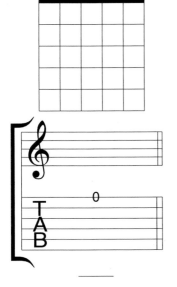

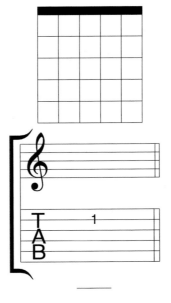

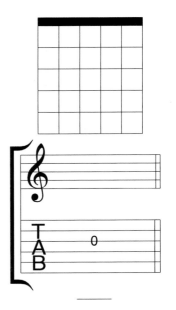

____

____

____

Use after page 16.

The Dotted Half Note

A **dot** placed after a note adds one-half the value of the original note. A dotted half note (𝅗𝅥·) equals 3 counts.

Write the beats under the notes:

New Time Signature: 3/4 Time

3 Three Counts To A Measure
4 A Quarter Note Receives One Count

In **3/4** time a half note receives two beats:

A quarter note receives one beat:

Write the beats under the notes. Remember, there are three beats in each measure.

Add the bar lines and name the notes of the following two musical excerpts.
End each line with a double bar.

Play the excerpts.

Use after page 20.

68

Two dots placed before a double bar line  means go back to the beginning and play again.

This is an excerpt from a well-known song:

Write the excerpt as it would appear **without** using a repeat sign.
(Some notes are indicated as a guide.)

Play the song. Can you name it?

New Note: A

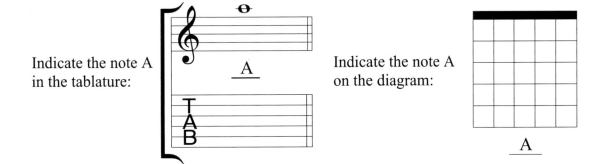

Indicate the note A in the tablature:

Indicate the note A on the diagram:

Country Trivia

Fill in the name of the performer and the composer.

On October 11th, 1975 _____ _____ 's recording of *Blue Eyes Crying in the Rain* climbed to #21 on the *Billboard* charts. It was recorded on the Columbia label. The music was written by _____ _____ and was first published in 1945. Its success again proves that a good song has lasting value. So, if you write one you really like, don't get discouraged if it doesn't become an overnight hit. This one reached stardom in Willie's interpretation thirty years after it was composed.

Use after page 21.

The Notes on the Fourth String

Name the notes indicated on the treble staff:

  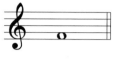

_____ _____ _____

This frame indicates a note played with the _____ finger at the _____ fret of the _____ string. Its note name is _____ . Play the note and say its name.

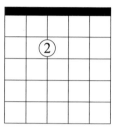

This tablature indication shows that the _____ string is to be played at the _____ fret. It will sound the note _____ . Play the note and say its name.

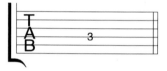

Name the notes indicated in the guitar frames:

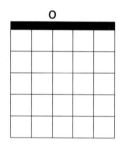 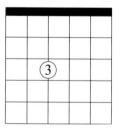

_____ _____

Draw the notes indicated in the tablature on the treble staves:

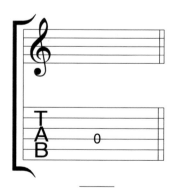  

_____ _____ _____

Name the notes and play them.

Use after page 26.

One eighth note looks like a quarter note with a flag added to its stem:

Groups of two or four eighth notes are joined by a beam: ♪♪ or ♪♪♪♪

Two eighth notes equal one quarter note: ♫ = ♩

Four eighth notes equal one half note: ♫♫ = ♩

Eight eighth notes eqaul one whole note: ♫♫♫♫ = o

In **4/4** time an eighth note receives 1/2 a beat:

1 & 2 & 3 & 4 &

Write the beats under the notes.

1 & 2 & 3 & 4 & _

Add the bar lines in the appropriate places. End with a double bar.

Add the beats:

♪ + ♪ = 1   ♫ + o =

♫ + ♩ =   ♩ + ♩ =

♩ + ♫ =   o + ♩ =

Draw the note value that equals the number of beats:

♪ + ♪ = ♩   ♩ + ♫ =

♫ + ♩ =   ♩ + ♩ =

Add the bar lines and name the notes in the following musical excerpt.

Play the excerpt.

Use after page 28.

Sharp Signs

A **sharp** sign (♯) raises the pitch of a note a half step.

When saying a sharp note's name, we say the letter name first and the sharp next—F sharp. When we write it on the music, the sharp sign comes first.

To draw a sharp, draw two vertical lines:	Then add the slanted lines:	Draw sharps before both F's:

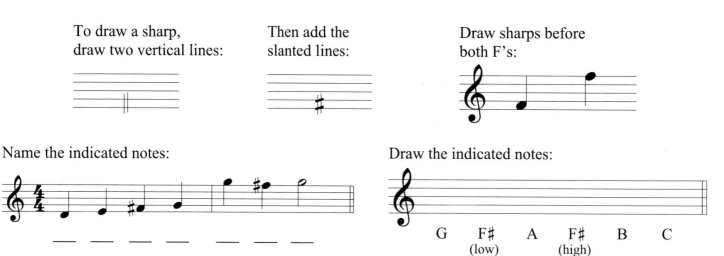

Name the indicated notes:

Draw the indicated notes:

G   F♯   A   F♯   B   C
(low)   (high)

Key Signature

When the F♯ is indicated at the beginning of the piece of music, it means every F in the piece is played F♯.

The key of G contains 1 sharp

Write the key signature for the key of G:

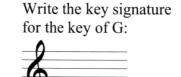

Name the notes:

___ ___ ___ ___ ___ ___ ___ ___ ___ ___ ___ ___ ___ ___

Rhythm Review

Fill in the missing beats with the appropriate notes. Each measure should contain 4 counts:

Fill in the missing beats with the appropriate notes. Each measure should contain 3 counts:

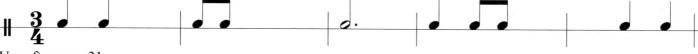

Use after page 31.

The C, G and G7 chords are illustrated on the chord frame diagrams. Draw the
indicated notes on the music staff.

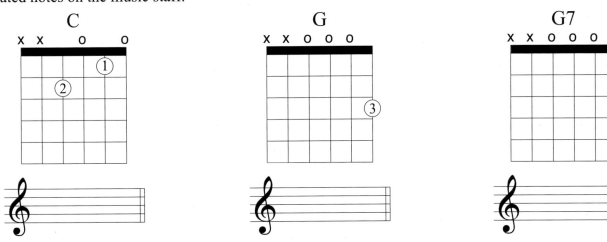

1. Notate, on the tablature, the chords indicated in the treble staff.
2. Name the chords.

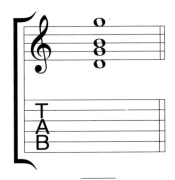
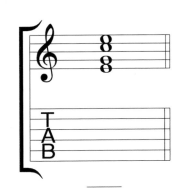

Fill in the chord frame diagrams to illustrate how the chords are fingered on the
guitar fretboard:

G7   C   G

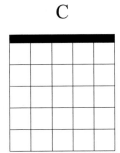
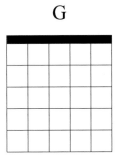

Use after page 32.

The D and D7 Chords

1. Notate, on the tablature, the chords indicated in the treble staff.
2. Name the chords.

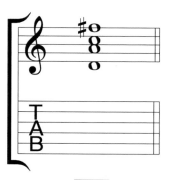

Fill in the chord frame diagrams to illustrate how the chords are fingered on the guitar fretboard:

D

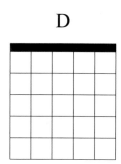

D7

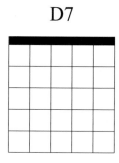

The D and D7 chords are illustrated on the chord frame diagrams below. Fill in the notes on the music staff.

D

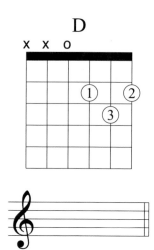

D7

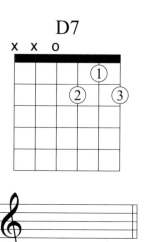

Use after page 33.

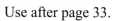

The 12-bar blues progression in the key of G uses the G, C and D chords. Sometimes the G7 and D7 are also used.

Fill in the chord frame diagrams to illustrate how the chords are fingered on the guitar fretboard. Then follow the rhythm slashes and play the *Down Home Blues*.

Down Home Blues

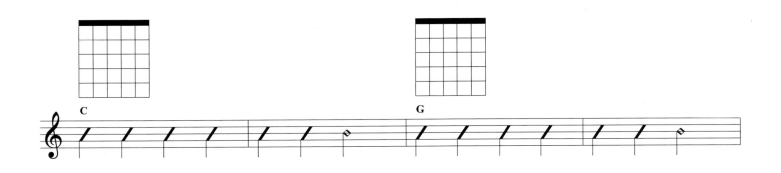

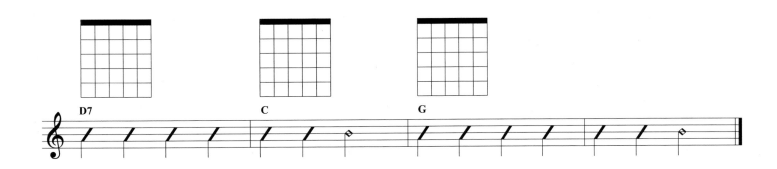

Use after page 34.

The Notes on the Fifth String

Name the indicated notes:

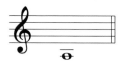 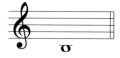 

_____ _____ _____

This frame indicates a note played with the _____ finger at the _____ fret of the _____ string. Its note name is _____ . Play the note and say its name.

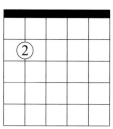

This tablature indication shows that the _____ string is to be played at the _____ fret. It will sound the note _____ . Play the note and say its name.

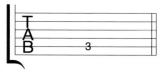

Name the notes indicated in the guitar frames:

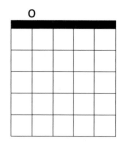 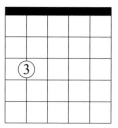

_____ _____

Draw the notes indicated in the tablature on the treble staves:

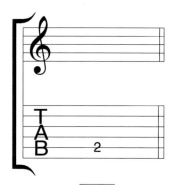  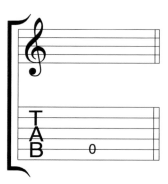

_____ _____ _____

Name the notes and play them.

Use after page 36.

The C (now in the full 5 string form), A minor and D minor chords are illustrated on the chord frame diagrams. Draw the indicated notes on the music staff.

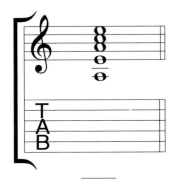

1. Notate, on the tablature, the chords indicated in the treble staff.
2. Name the chords.

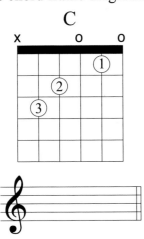

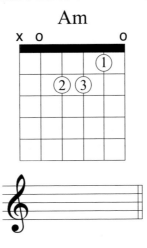

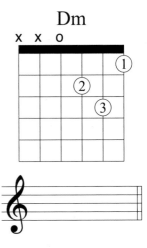

Fill in the chord frame diagrams to illustrate how the chords are fingered on the guitar fretboard:

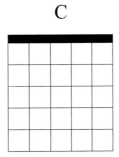

C

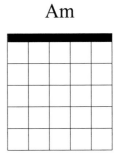

Use after page 38.

1. Notate, on the tablature, the chords indicated in the treble staff.
2. Name the chords.

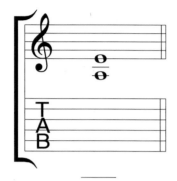

Fill in the chord frame diagrams to illustrate how the chords are fingered on the guitar fretboard:

D5

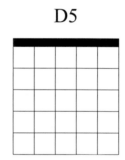

A5

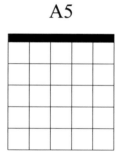

The power chords A5 and D5 are illustrated in the following chord frame diagrams. Draw the indicated notes on the music staff.

A5

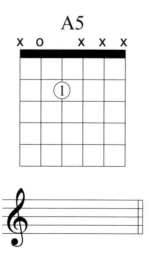

D5

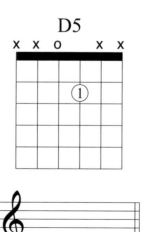

Use after page 44.

The repeat sign tells you to go back to the beginning. On the repeat, skip the first ending and play the second ending.

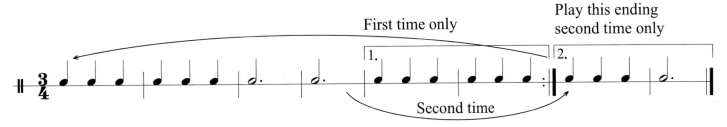

Write this piece of music as it would appear without the first and second endings:

Now go back and play the song.

Chord Review

Name the chords and notate them in the tablature:

Use after page 45.

The Notes on the Sixth String

Name the notes:

_____   _____   _____

This frame indicates a note played with the _____ finger at the ___ fret of the ___ string. Its note name is _____ . Play the note and say its name.

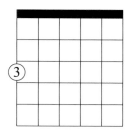

This tablature indication shows that the ___ string is to be played at the _____ fret. It will sound the note _____ . Play the note and say its name.

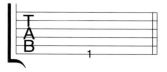

Name the notes indicated in the guitar frames:

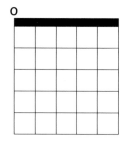 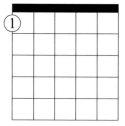

_____   _____

Draw the notes indicated in the tablature:

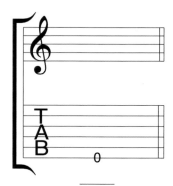 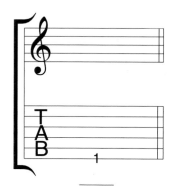 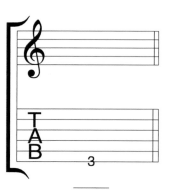

_____   _____   _____

Name the notes and play them.

Use after page 46.

The E5 power chord is illustrated on the chord frame diagram.

1. Draw the notes indicated on the staff.
2. Notate the chord in the tablature.
3. Name the chord.
4. Play the chord.

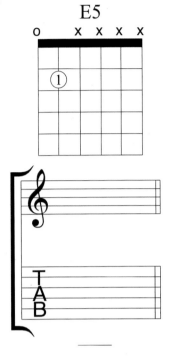

Power Chord Review

The A5 and D5 power chords are illustrated on the chord frame diagrams.

1. Draw the notes on the staff.
2. Notate the chord in the tablature.
3. Name the chord.
4. Play the chord.

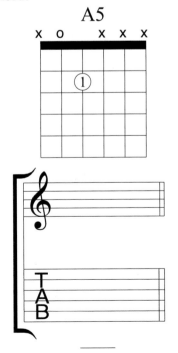

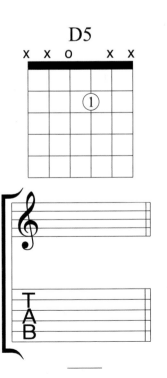

Use after page 50.

This rock blues uses three power chords: A5, D5 and E5.

Fill in the chord frame diagrams to illustrate how the chords are fingered on the guitar fretboard. Then follow the rhythm slashes and play *Getting The Feel*. Use P.M. throughout and play all accents.

Getting the Feel

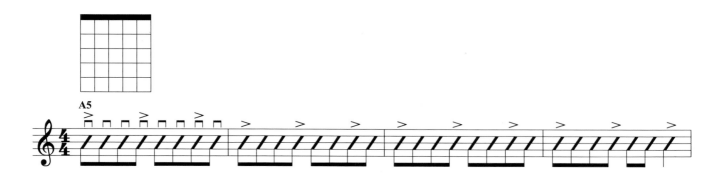

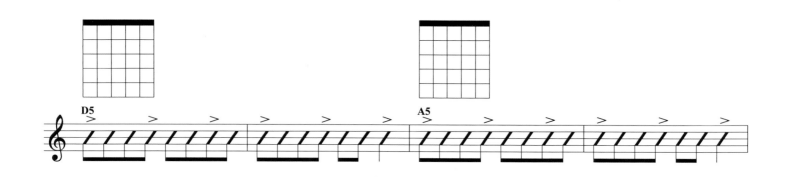

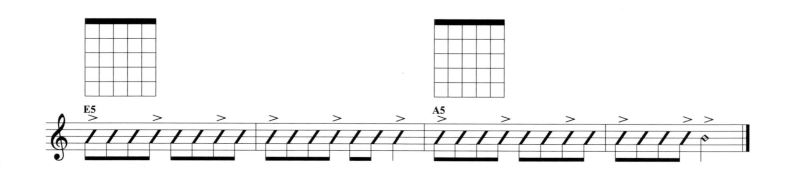

Use after page 51.

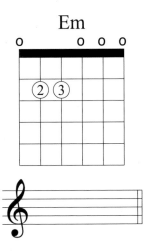

The full G, G7 and E minor chords are illustrated on the chord frame diagrams.
Draw the indicated notes on the music staff.

G

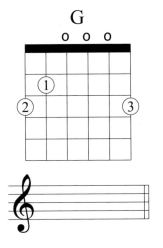

G7

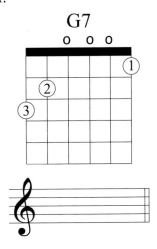

Em

1. Notate, on the tablature, the chords indicated in the treble staff.
2. Name the chords.

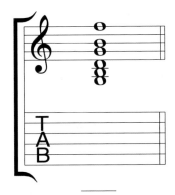

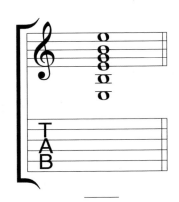

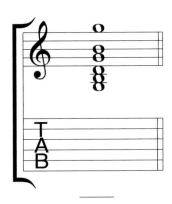

_____

_____

_____

Fill in the chord frame diagrams to illustrate how the chords are fingered on the guitar fretboard:

Em

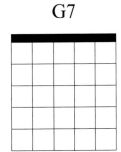

G7

G

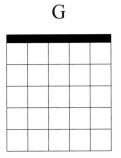

Use after page 52.

Fill in the name of the indicated note:

This frame indicates a note played with the _____ finger at the ___ fret of the ___ string. Its note name is _____ . Play the note and say its name.

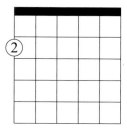

This tablature indication shows that the ___ string is to be played at the _____ fret. It will sound the note _____ . Play the note and say its name.

Note Review

Name the notes, then play them:

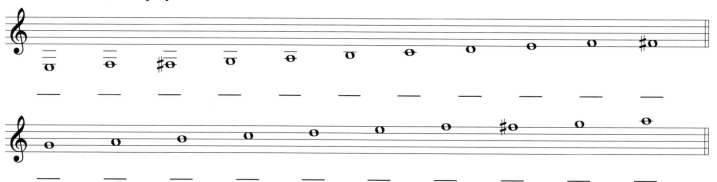

Rhythm Review

Add the bar lines, then clap the rhythm:

Use after page 53.

The duration of musical silence is indicated by different types of rests.

In **4/4** time a whole rest receives four beats:

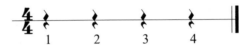

A half rest receives two beats:

A quarter rest receives one beat:

An eighth rest receives 1/2 of a beat:

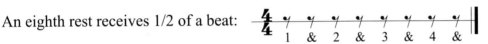

In the next exercise, fill in the missing beats with rests. Use only one rest in each measure, then clap the rhythm.

Add the bar lines, then clap the rhythm:

Fill in the blanks:

One whole rest equals _____ beats.
One quarter rest equals _____ beat.
One half rest equals _____ beats.

Use after page 55.

The E6, A6 and D6 power chords are illustrated on the chord frame diagrams.
Draw the indicated notes on the music staff.

E6

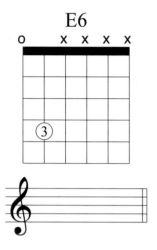

A6

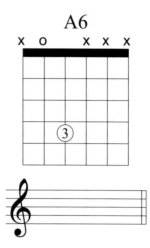

D6

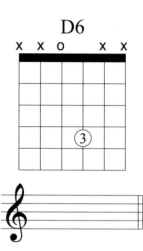

1. Notate, on the tablature, the chords indicated in the treble staff.
2. Name the chords.

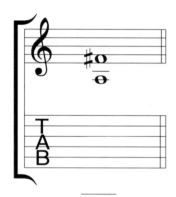

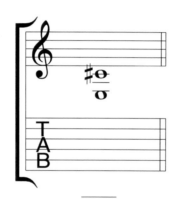

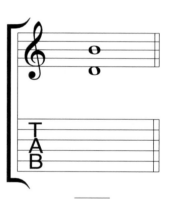

Fill in the chord frame diagrams to illustrate how the chords are fingered on the guitar fretboard:

D6

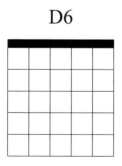

E6

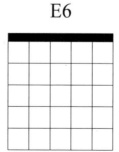

A6

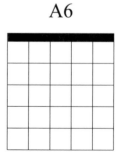

Use after page 56.

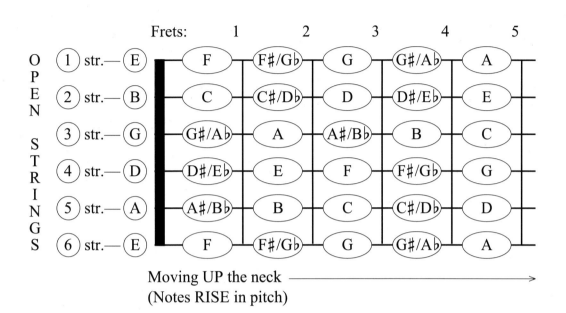

Moving UP the neck ⟶
(Notes RISE in pitch)

Guitar Chord Chart

Indicate the correct fingerings at the correct frets to complete this chord chart.

Am
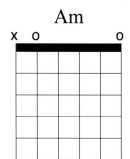

B7
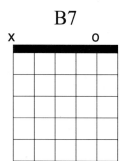

C
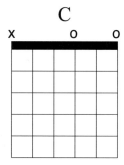

D
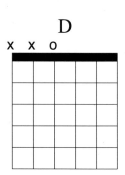

Dm
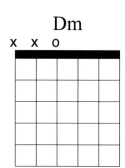

D7
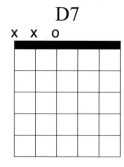

Em
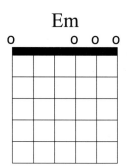

G
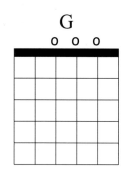

G7
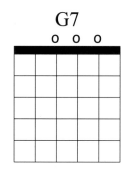

A5
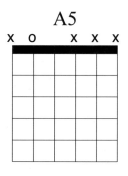

D5
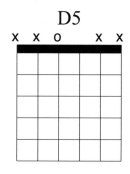

E5
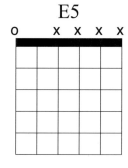

A6
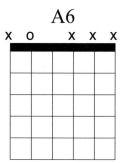

D6
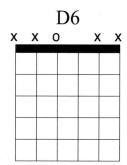

E6
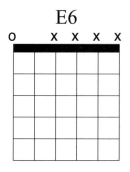